A Promise Kept

A Promise Kept

❖

The Story of One Widowed Bride's Journey through Grief

Elise Crawford

Library of Congress Control Number: 2009901185
ISBN: Hardcover   978-1-4415-1039-6
                     Softcover   978-1-4415-1038-9

This book was printed in the United States of America.

The Prayer
Words and Music by Carole Bayer Sager and David Foster
Italian Lyric by Alberto Testa and Tony Renis
© 1996 Warner-Tamerlane Publishing Corp. and WB Music Corp.
All rights reserved. Used by permission.

Time in a Bottle
Words and Music by Jim Croce
© 1972 Denjac Music Company. © Renewed 2000 and assigned to Croce
Publishing in the USA.
All rights outside the USA administered by Denjac Music Company.
All rights reserved. Used by permission.

The Morning After
(from "The Poseidon Adventure")
Words and Music by Al Kasha and Joel Hirschhorn
© 1972 (Renewed) WB Music Corp. and Warner-Tamerlane Publishing Corp.
All rights reserved. Used by permission.

Amazing Grace by John Newton, Vern Adams, and Wilbur Jones
© by Peermusic Ltd.
Used by permission. All rights reserved.

To order additional copies of this book, contact:
Xlibris Corporation
1-888-795-4274
www.Xlibris.com
Orders@Xlibris.com
57964

A Promise Kept

In memory of Mark Francis McLaughlin
June 13, 1954-November 27, 1998

For Roberto Martinez, you made it your mission that I take the first steps toward acceptance, toward healing. You would not take no for an answer, and for that, I am thankful. You taught me how to grieve and let myself grieve. You freed me to live, to love, and to attach again and empowered me to believe in myself and in this book. Because of you, I can trust, love, and be loved again. Love can happen twice. I love you so much.

For Barry Samet, you were my beacon and salvation during the storm of the most trying time in my life. You did not forget us nor sweep us under the rug. You have positively influenced our lives with your kindness and generosity. You sought every opportunity to help me stand right again. I will always be grateful for the tribute you gave to Mark, for all the recognition he has received, and for the special friend you have become to me and my children. Because of you and all of your efforts, Mark will never be forgotten.

Publishing of A Promise Kept
was made possible in part by the many
customers of CEDAR-AL cedar oil products
at www.cedaroil.com.
Thank You.

Acknowledgments

I am eternally indebted to all those who have traveled this journey with me: our Heavenly Father; Lexi and Dale; Jenny (Jennifer Bradley) and Jiahna; Mommy, Roberto, and Lucky; David Moorhead (Lexi's beau and photographer for the cover of *A Promise Kept*); Ralph Winamaki; Barbara Gardner; the Seattle Milk Fund; the employees—my former coworkers—executives, and council members of King County; the DOT;, Metro and Local 587; Barry and Sandy Samet; Rick Walsh; Wayne Huston; Bonnie Hanson; Les Hoffman; Josh Shields; Kenny McCormick; Ron Sims; Virginia Mason Medical Center—coworkers and employees; all local news channels; the Seferos family; Stephanie Mann; Lisa and her husband; the Embassy Suites Hotel; the Spangler Candy Company; Dawes Transport; Randy and Evelyn Smith; Work Source—Fred, Rita, and John; Pace Staffing Network; the YMCA—Shoreline; all the directors, managers, and coworkers of Nutro Products—PetCo and PetSmart; Providence Everett-Norm and Rita; Karen, Stan, Fred, Pastor Don, and the Church of the Good Shepherd; Gary and Dominque; Jim and Mary; Joan and Gerald Oncken; Stop Watch Espresso-Shauna and Andy; Wolfgang Treppens; and Dianne and Mark Greenhouse.

A heartfelt appreciation to the rescuers who responded to the accident scene: media relations; West, North, South, and East 2nd and 3rd watch; parking enforcement; special operations;

communications; domestic violence; homicide; robbery; accident investigations units; companies—E2, 8, 9, 17, 18, 20, 22, and 25; L4, 7, and 9; B4, 5, and 6; A2, 14, 17; M1, 16, 28, 31, 63, 44, and 33; Air9, Staff 10, Power 25, and Saft 2—and the countless citizens who were there helping as well.

A world full of gratitude to those who prayed for us and sent us their condolences. You have made my journey bearable and possible: all public transportation organizations nationwide, RTA-ATU brothers and sisters, School District Transportation Association, Pacific Northwest citizens and Metro riders, all Metro bases employees, Stan Green, Gunner Goelitz, Dave Kidder, Mary Peterson, Mary Collins, Roy Harrington—to whom we'll be forever grateful for his efforts in making Sweet Thursday a reality, Paul Toliver, Marc Walsh, Jim LaSala, Jim Patrick, Terry Compton, Ray Coffey, Patti Hardin, Governor Gary Locke, US Senator Patty Murray, Oprah, BSA Troop 332 and Janet Way, Tim-Tammy-Erin Gensch, Tony-Rita-Disco, Hilltop Elementary School, the staff at KUOW, the Bixenman and Graham families, Cleveland White for his drawing, the Hendrix family, my former Lynnwood neighbors for all of their generosity, John T. Farrell, Janet Palmer, *The Seattle Times* and *The Seattle Post—Intelligencer, Dateline, Northwest Afternoon,* Men Without Kilts S Lasses Fair, King County Sheriff's Honor Guard, the Greater Seattle Pipe Band, and Bob and Robin at Audio Visual Specialists.

And finally, I would like to acknowledge Stephen S. Howie—Lecturer, Journalism Department, Western Washington University—and Alan J. Kaufman, publishing attorney, for their guidance. I would also like to thank the countless others who have directly or indirectly walked this journey with me; through each of you, my burden has been lighter and the journey bearable. May God always bless and bring love to each of you.

Introduction

(Author's Note: Some names and detailed descriptions of certain characters in this story have been withheld to protect the identity of the sources.)

*T*his isn't a happy-ever-after story. It is about my process through grief. *A Promise Kept* is written in a four-part journey exploring the true story of how—as an independent, economically challenged young single mother—I lost my heart to a gentle giant driving a Seattle Metro bus, how it seemed to end following his brutal murder in an unprovoked act of violence, and how it began anew on a famous bridge in Seattle. In the telling of my story, I take on several roles: as the narrator, as the one affected by the heartbreaking tragedy, and as an observer. In the various roles, I am referred to by several names derived from the name I was given at birth—Elisa. Before the tragedy, friends and family called me Lissie or Lis for short; both are spelled with an *s* but pronounced with a *z*. And during the past eight years, everyone else has called me Elise.

The first chapter will pull you into my nightmare as I describe the life-altering paradox of that fateful day, November 27, 1998, in several chaotic scenes. With a systematic investigation into facts and theories, I reconstructed the tragedy of that day, in perfect detail, in hopes that by reliving *my experience*, you will relive your own. In the second chapter, I retreat nine years prior to the tragedy and bring our love story alive with such clarity that you will understand why his loss affected me so profoundly. Then, in the following chapters, I return to the day after the tragedy and begin journaling my spiraling descent into hell through a complex system of paths, obstacles—including the tragic death of my mother—and betrayals through which I inevitably become lost, essentially *missing* for nearly eight years in a labyrinthine maze of grief. It is only with courageousness, fortitude, and faith—holding fast to my beloved's memory—that I am guided through the long and arduous labyrinth to eventually find my way *home*, to be with my loved ones once again.

Although our experiences may be very different, I hope that by sharing my true feelings, raw emotions, and mental anguish I suffered needlessly while making my own way down that road less traveled—the journey of grief—my struggles are just enough for you to relate to, to help you to heal, and to seek hope from; and that they would encourage you to keep going forward and not give up. Above all, I hope for you to know that what you are experiencing is normal, that you aren't crazy, and that stifled grief can hurt you. I hope that by removing my superficial mask and exposing all that I've hidden away—the ugly, the harsh, and the negative—by no means perfectly, eloquently, or maturely—and by experiencing my pain and crying along with me, you will come away with the courage needed to face, to *accept,* and to begin your own journey regardless of what kind of loss you've had.

I pray you will find some relief from the grief monster that dwells inside of your own heart, preventing your first steps. If my story makes a difference in at least one person's life, then the pain of my loss was not in vain. I grieve. I cry. I am fearful. I am strong. Through faith in our Heavenly Father, we will find the courage to move forward together.

I wish you peace.

Elise Crawford

I've included a bonus story as the last chapter in this book. It is the first short story I wrote prior to the writing of this book. It is a story about an angelic gift in the form of a little kitten that cheats death and brings hope to a grieving family.

Chapter One: November 27, 1998

The Prayer

I pray you'll be our eyes and watch us where we go
And help us to be wise in times when we don't know.
Let this be our prayer when we lose our way
Leadustotheplace,guideuswithyourgracetoaplacewherewe'llbesafe;
The light that you give us; I pray we'll find your light
Will stay in our hearts and hold it in our hearts
Reminding us when stars go out each night
That in my prayer you are the everlasting star
Let this be our prayer
There's so much faith when shadows fill our day
Lead us to a place; guide us with your grace
Give us faith so we'll be safe
We dream of a world with no more violence
A world of justice and hope
Grasp your neighbor's hand as a symbol of peace and
brotherhood
The strength that you give us
We ask that life be kind is the wish
And watch us from above
That everyone may find love
We hope each soul will find in and around himself another soul
to love
Let this be our prayer; let this be our prayer
Just like every child; just like every child
Need to find a place, guide us with your grace
Give us faith so we'll be safe
And the faith that you've lit inside us I feel will save us.

More relatives visited that year than before. Choosing to ignore the reality and seriousness of her fate, Mark's mom went about dinner like she did every year—smiling, laughing, and joking—with not a care in the world. The kids played with the other relatives while the adults visited. Everything was as it usually was. And what we thought was going to be a solemn Thanksgiving turned out to be one of the better ones. Because Mark and I had to work the following day, it was decided that Lexi would stay the night with his mom and his sister. So with a final round of hugs and kisses for all, Mark, the boys, and I headed for home. As we drove, I couldn't help but think how devastated and depressed Mark was going to be without his mom, and how learning to live without her was to be our greatest challenge yet . . .

Ground Zero

$\mathcal{U}$p early, I went through my usual morning routine to prepare for one last day of work before the holiday weekend. Mark's shift started later than mine, which allowed him more time for shut-eye. Ready to leave, I stopped to kiss him goodbye. Feigning sleep, he startled me when he grabbed my arms and pulled me toward him. Laughing, I pried myself from his arms, and he reluctantly let me go. We quickly went over the plan for the children for the day. Lexi would remain with his sister and mom, and then I would pick her up on my way home from work. His oldest would be working until late; his youngest would be staying home alone, and Dale would go to work with him. I left with his promise to call me on his break.

Mark and Dale were about to leave the house when my sister, Jenny, who lived on the opposite side of town from us, was suddenly awakened from a sound sleep.

*   *   *

Like the vicious and loud beating of jungle drums, her heart pounded so intensely that it woke her from a sound sleep. Still caught up in the nightmare that she just couldn't shake, she sat straight up in bed. Half awake, her mind tried desperately to make some sense of it. Shaking her to the core of her very soul, she had one consistent, loud, and overwhelming thought. She had to get her nephew, Dale. Trembling, she fumbled in the darkness of her room for the phone and called her sister's house.

*   *   *

Mark and Dale were about to climb into the truck when they heard the phone ring. Mark hesitated but decided that there was enough time and went to answer it. It was my sister, Jenny. She was crying hysterically. She insisted that she be allowed to pick up Dale. She begged Mark to leave him at home and that she would explain it to me later. Confused by her irrational behavior but without time to argue or to call me at work, he agreed to leave Dale at home. And without another word, before he could even say goodbye, he heard her hang up.

Forgetting to put on her coat, Jenny flew out the door in her pajamas, her heart still pounding a million times per second. Like a wild woman, with makeup from the night before now smeared down her face from the tears she'd been crying and her hair a tangled mess, she jumped into her car and raced for my house. When she finally reached Dale, she grabbed him into her arms, hugged him tightly, and cried harder than she ever cried before. Realizing that she confused and frightened him with her appearance and behavior, she could only explain that she had had a bad dream and just wanted him to visit her for the day.

At 10:00 AM, I called home to assure that Mark had taken Dale to work with him. Mark's son told me that Jenny had picked up Dale instead. I just couldn't believe it. Mark knew we never went against *the plan* without talking it over first. I was irritated. I couldn't wait until he called me, on his break, to see just what kind of reason he had for letting Dale go with her. Mark called me at work just before 2:30 PM. He said that there was a reasonable explanation for deviating from the plan, but because he was a little late leaving from Aurora Village to downtown, he would have to fill me in after he got home. Irritated or not, for the time being, I had to settle for his brief explanation. I wished him—as I always did—"Drive safe. I love you" and let him go back to work. I was not looking forward to the inevitable confrontation with my sister that was sure to follow when I picked Dale up later.

Mark's seventy-two-foot passenger-articulated diesel bus trundled southbound on Aurora Avenue North, stopping periodically for passengers amid the strip malls, motels, and parking lots. Several boarded with Christmas packages from shopping, and others were on their way into town for more shopping. Some boarded for a spontaneous journey just glad to be outside after a week of pouring rain. Some were just glad to be off their feet after a long work shift and looked forward to settling in for a brief nap during the ride home while others headed to work. Some passengers read while others visited quietly with each other. It was an unusually quiet ride even with thirty-two passengers on board. The seats were occupied in no particular order, and only one passenger chose to sit up front across from the driver, the very seat Dale would have occupied had he gone to work with Mark. As the bus approached the Aurora Bridge, the passenger sitting closest to Mark stood up and approached him as if he were going to ask a question. But the man didn't say a word. He pulled out a gun, pointed it at Mark, and shot him twice in his side instead.

It happened so fast that Mark didn't have time to hit the emergency alarm. The man grabbed the steering wheel. Mark fought him, struggling to stay conscious and in control of the bus. The once-lulling quiet was shattered by their confrontation. There were more popping sounds from the gun. A passenger in the back yelled, "Gun! Gun!" In a panic, riders fell to their knees and covered their heads. Before losing consciousness, Mark pushed on the brakes as hard as he could, leaving a permanent scar on the pavement. His firm grip lessened, and he slumped unconscious over the steering wheel. The bus continued onward. It veered left and skidded another one hundred feet before going out of control. The bus swerved into the northbound oncoming traffic, traveling forty-nine miles per hour. It hit a van, crushing it all the way to its bumper, and then jumped a fifteen-inch curb and slammed into a guardrail. Grinding metal against metal and concrete, the bus ripped through a twenty-five-foot section of the rail and barreled right into a light pole, bending it in half. And then bus 359 flew off the Aurora Bridge.

*   *   *

Attributes of a Bus Driver

*M*ark was both friendly and entertaining with his passengers. He was a practical jokester professionally as well as personally. He believed that people were too serious sometimes and needed a good laugh once in a while. So he took it upon himself and made an unwritten addendum to his job description. It was his daily goal to make as many people smile as he could. One of the ways in which he demonstrated this—in an especially entertaining fashion—was with his overhead microphone, which was used to announce the arrival of an upcoming destination. It was expected that whenever he approached a transit center, it would be announced as the "transient center."

For the adult's entertainment, he often wore a funny—yet some would say controversial—button pinned to the lapel of his shirt. The buttons would either start a conversation or be reciprocated with a glare. Although some of the buttons were confiscated by his boss, it only added fuel to the fire and gave Mark one more reason to wear others just like them. Little did unsuspecting passengers realize that Mark kept notes, to himself, of the reactions he got for the antics he

Chapter One: November 27, 1998

performed that day. If they were received well enough, he made sure to use those same ones again in the near future. For the children, with parental approval, he always had candy; and at Christmas time, he gave the children authentic, one-of-a-kind candy canes. There wasn't a bus-riding child in Seattle who didn't like him.

With or without a captive audience, Mark saw the newly built underground bus tunnels, in downtown Seattle, as an opportunity to transform his bus into a roller coaster. He drove through them at breakneck speeds like a bat out of hell. And as he drove willy-nilly, with a huge wad of Bazooka bubble gum in his mouth, he'd blow the biggest bubble he could, open the driver-side window—his long hair lashing around wildly—aim with careful precision for a specific direction sign, and spit the gum at it as hard as he could. His disgusting display of art was still there the last time I passed through.

I empathized with the person who had to clean up after his obscenely gross masterpiece. Whenever I happened to be along for the ride, if there were passengers that were witness to his insane behavior, I would avoid eye contact with them and keep my eyes averted until they finally left the bus. You can just imagine what they thought. And you can bet—more often than not—his antics would end up on complaint forms that awaited his next return to the bus base sometimes on a weekly basis. But with little more than a slap on the hand, they didn't go much farther than that. And for awhile afterward, he would let up a little with his pranks, but it wasn't long before he was back in full swing with more entertaining—or irritating (depending on how one saw it)—antics to entertain the public. He was just that way. If he knew something about him bothered you—either in the way he dressed, spoke, or behaved—he would continue doing whatever it was just to irritate you even further. I wasn't sure if this side of him was more maniacal or adoring.

*   *   *

Somebody yelled, "Oh my god! Were going off . . ." Passengers braced themselves for the impact, certain that they were going to die. Mark's airborne bus fell as if in slow motion some forty feet to the ground. The sleepy little neighborhood, with twentieth-century homes, was changed forever by what happened next. The front end of the bus smashed onto the entry level of a two-story apartment complex. Sliding down the side of the tenement, the bus tore through evergreen trees and ripped off porches and stairways on its way down. Mark, not buckled into his seat, was ejected headfirst through the windshield and onto the roof of the building. Like the sound of five garbage trucks hitting the ground at the same time, the forty-thousand-pound bus landed hard on the front lawn of the dwelling. Mostly in one piece, it wrapped itself around a tree, in a V shape, before coming to rest practically in the lap of Mark's beloved Fremont Troll. Big chunks of concrete followed its decent, showering everything and anyone below with a swirl of glass, metal, and blood. People were screaming, seats were breaking, and seventy-five gallons of diesel fuel was spilling everywhere from a ruptured fuel tank. The exact location was fateful. Five seconds later, it would have plunged more than one hundred feet into Lake Union.

An occupant of the apartment building was sitting on his front porch when the bus passed overhead. Another was taking a shower when he suddenly felt the building move. He grabbed on to the sides of the shower and braced himself for what he thought was *the big one*. He rushed, dripping wet, from the bathroom and grabbed some clothes. Looking toward his front door, he was stunned to see that it had been jarred open. Approaching cautiously, he looked outside to find that his front porch was gone. Looking down, he stared right into the frightened faces of people trapped inside of a broken bus. Just a few feet away, another resident—witnessing the frightening scene—made the sign of the cross and prayed, "God help them."

The First Call for Emergency Services

At 3:09 PM, the call went in. "Nine-one-one, what are you reporting?" The caller hysterically screamed into the phone, "A bus has gone over the Aurora Bridge and has landed in my yard! People are crawling out of the bus windows!"

West, East, South, and North precincts are radioed to respond to the scene. All enforcement agencies are ordered to stand by for possible mutual aide. Ten off-duty firefighters, five medic units, and twenty-seven aid vehicles had already arrived at the scene. Emergency vehicles, everything from ladder trucks to technical rescue teams, crowded the narrow streets. The quiet little neighborhood soon became a mini—war zone. Sirens filled the air; orders were screamed out among the rescuers.

The injured, twisted and scattered about like dolls, could be heard crying and moaning for help. The smell of diesel fuel soaked the air. The threat of a massive explosion was imminent. Onlookers became rescuers, sixty-five in all, and others looters. The rescuers worked to pry the front doors of the bus while terrified passengers pushed frantically from within to force them open. The doors eventually gave way, allowing dozens of paramedics and firefighters to work quickly to pull bleeding riders out of the shattered bus. Several injured passengers lay piled up in the stairwell. One rescuer yelled repeatedly into the bus, "Where's the driver? Has anyone seen the driver?" An injured passenger managed to answer, "The driver's been shot. Somebody shot the driver several times!" The interior of the bus was saturated with diesel fuel. It flowed onto the ground and down the street, spreading diesel fumes throughout the scene. It coated the interior of the bus, the victims, and the rescuers, making their efforts difficult and dangerous.

Firefighters and Other Emergency Personnel Respond

Outside the bus, firefighters worked frantically to connect hoses to nearby fire hydrants. Just west of the bus, a generator and lights were set up. Even more firefighters worked above the scene, at top of the bridge, tying off a part of the east guardrail and the light pole that had been dangling precariously over the side. Other rescue teams searched the apartment building for casualties. They found none, only minor injuries. Any remaining tenants were evacuated. Firefighters investigating the building decided to disconnect the electricity. Working quickly, and using whatever force necessary, they entered each apartment that wasn't structurally damaged or unsafe and flipped the circuit breakers off. A dog team searched the entire scene for victims who may have wandered off and collapsed, but no additional victims were found.

At the bottom of the pile was a passenger suffering from a head injury with massive bleeding. Another passenger's head was stuck in the undercarriage of the bus. The Jaws of Life was brought in to free him. Some of the critically injured passengers were placed onto backboards and lifted out of the side windows. One victim's body was caught half in and half out of the bus. His upper body lay on the floor while the lower half hung out of the ripped-open side of the bus. Someone pulled the victim all the way out and put him on the ground. Another passenger's leg bone was sticking out the side of his pant leg; his screams were deafening as a medical team worked to put it into a splint. Miraculously, some passengers were relatively unhurt and able to walk out the front door.

News Coverage: Just After 3:00 PM

*J*ust after 3:00 PM this afternoon, a bus started onto the Aurora Bridge, a six-lane roadway spanning Seattle's ship canal, when suddenly several loud pops were heard, and the bus jerked violently. The bus veered to the left, out of control, and at full speed, it careened across three lanes of oncoming traffic, hitting a van then clipping a lamppost before plowing through a concrete barrier. It then dropped some forty-five feet, bouncing off an apartment building roof before crashing to the ground below. Somehow, the twenty-ton vehicle landed on its wheels in a broken heap with every one of its passengers injured, many critically. Within minutes, a major rescue effort was under way.

A police officer approached a minimally hurt victim and asked if he had witnessed the shooting. The passenger said he had and described the shooter as a white male in his forties, six-feet-two-inches tall, 190-200 lbs, wearing a tan hat and coat, dark glasses, and possibly carrying a bag of some sort. The officer asked the passenger if he would walk around the scene with him in an attempt to locate the suspect. The passenger agreed. Thoroughly searching the entire area as well as the crowd of onlookers, he could not identify the suspect.

News Coverage: The Rescue Is So Massive

*T*he rescue is so massive it is straining the limits of the Seattle Fire Department. Bystanders have become rescuers. I've been told there are at least two citizens to every victim. Firefighters have said they are making the rescue a success.

Firefighter: Hollywood Can't Script

*H*ollywood can't script some of the things we respond to, so we're always thinking of a worst-case scenario. We've never seen anything like this. This is a once-in-a-career type call. There's no question, we were like oh my god what do we have here. We had numerous civilians coming at us from all directions, yelling that people needed our help, and they were all pointing in several different directions. People were in the stairwell of the bus, upside down, on top of each other, arms and legs going all over the place.

Outside of the bus, bodies were strewn in the driving area as well as the yard of the apartment building. Rescuers did not find the driver among them. The horrific tragedy soon turned into a homicide investigation. Police officially took over and began to search for the driver. They cordoned off a large area and posted officers to guard the scene. More officers were sent to establish containment for crowd and traffic control so that rescue vehicles could leave with the injured.

News Pilot: The Area of the Tragedy

*T*he area of the tragedy scene remains unstable, the Aurora Bridge remains closed, and drivers will have to take an alternate route. As you can see, if the bus had fallen just one hundred yards farther south of the scene, just ten

seconds later, it would have fallen over one hundred feet or
ten stories into the canal. There likely wouldn't have been
any survivors, it could have been much worse. As well, you
can see traffic from all around is backed up for miles. It's
going to be a long night for those stuck in the traffic.

A firefighter paramedic arrived on the scene. He put on an
orange-colored vest with the word Triage written on it in large letters
and went to work, sorting the injured victims. His job was both simple
and agonizing. He had to decide who needed immediate help, who
could wait, and who was beyond help. A quick look or a hand on the
chest measured respiratory rate; a flick of the fingers on the wrist found
both pulse and blood pressure to determine if a victim was bleeding
out; and some quick, simple questions gauged mental status.

News Coverage: It's Like a Scene from a Disaster Movie

*I*t's like a scene from a disaster movie. A seventy-two-
foot passenger-articulated diesel bus lays jackknifed and
cracked open after a horrifying plunge off a bridge.
Witnesses say they ran for their lives. Survivors of the
crash say there were people screaming.

Each assessment took approximately five seconds. If a victim
failed one of the tests, a red ribbon was wrapped around his arm for
priority treatment and taken immediately to the hospital. Walking
wounded or uninjured, green tags; serious but responsive, yellow
tags. Those not breathing got one last chance. If they didn't breathe
and/or were beyond help at the scene, black tags. Nearly three-fourths
were tagged with red ribbon. Once tagged, each victim was assigned a
number. A police officer was standing by the final victim the firefighter
had to assess. He was told the man fit the description of the suspect. The
victim was covered in dirt and blood. He had dark circles around both
of his eyes indicative of a head wound. He had a light pulse and was
barely breathing. Upon further inspection, he found what appeared

to be a single gunshot wound to the man's head. They searched his body for a weapon but were unable to find one. They intubated the victim and continued to breathe for him as they strapped him to a backboard. A red ribbon was tied around his arm, and one of the waiting ambulances took him immediately to the hospital.

Rescuers Worked in Relay

*R*escuers worked in relay. IV tubing was untangled and prepared. O2 bottles, C-collars, tape, and ringers were all prepared and made ready as fast as they were needed. CPR was performed on a bleeding victim, and a breathing tube was inserted down his throat. Another was assisted with his breathing by a ventilating bag. As fast as humanly possible, vitals were taken and recorded, injuries were bandaged and summarized, and then victims were strapped onto a backboard and loaded into waiting ambulances. Local area hospitals emptied beds as fast as they could for the influx of incoming casualties. A command officer on the phone with a doctor from Harborview Medical Center received directions: I have two yellows and a red, "Go to Swedish . . ." I have three yellows, "Go to Ballard . . ."

*   *   *

About 3:30 PM, a friend of mine called me at work. I could tell by the sound of her voice that she was upset. "What route is Mark driving today? Was he going to be traveling on Aurora?" I answered that he was substituting on the route 6, and that "Yes, he would be traveling on Aurora. Why?" She said, "There has been a terrible accident . . ." I didn't hear the rest of what she said. My heart pounded loudly in my ears; I suddenly had tunnel vision and felt very sick. My stomach turned and twisted. I felt I would vomit. I felt freezing cold, and yet I was perspiring. The room seemed to close in. I felt like I was suffocating. I reached for my purse and searched frantically for my inhaler. I took a couple of puffs, but it didn't help. I still couldn't catch my breath.

*   *   *

A firefighter looked up at the apartment building and noticed a pair of legs dangling and not moving over the side of the building. A rescue team grabbed a ladder and their equipment and supplies. They carefully approached the injured person. They recognized the familiar uniform and knew at once they had found the missing bus driver.

*   *   *

Mark

*M*ark loved his family—above all, his mother. He loved music, mostly '80s pop. He liked U2 the most, especially their album *Achtung Baby*—from which he dedicated nearly every song to me. He also liked the Cure, Depeche Mode, Oingo Boingo, Devo, and New Radicals just to name a few. But of all of them, Jimi Hendrix was closest to his heart. He loved the British comedian John Cleese, especially when he played Basil on the show *Fawlty Towers*. Sometimes he referred endearingly to me as Sybil, Basil's wife on the program. He loved the movie *The Fisher King*; he was especially fond of Robin Williams. But his all-time favorite movie was *The Wizard of Oz*.

He liked to play basketball and baseball outside of work, mostly with some of his bus-driver buddies, yet he didn't care to watch them on TV. He loved the hot-air-balloon season—the crazier the shapes, the better—and photography. His camera was always at the ready to take a picture. Some photos he had enlarged and framed while others he made into collages and gave away as gifts. His favorite liquor was tequila, but he enjoyed an occasional beer as well. His greatest downfall was Coca-Cola—much to his dentist's disapproval—it was rare to see him without a thirty-two ounce Big Gulp in his hand. He loved dim sum of which he would partake whenever he visited his Canadian relatives. He loved sweets, especially Twinkies and Ho Hos, and proudly proclaimed that he could eat a whole one in a single bite.

Mark with rescuers

The slow descend of Mark's body

Those who tried to save him

Chapter One: November 27, 1998

He loved rocky-road ice cream and cookies of any kind but never anything made with coconut. His breakfast of choice was Cocoa Puffs. For lunch, he absolutely loved ampm cheeseburgers. For dinner, he usually passed up what the family had and ate a huge bowl of popcorn instead. If anyone ever suggested a healthier diet, he would tell them, "I didn't get this big eating that crap!"

In a nutshell, Mark was a gentle giant. He stood out in a crowd, and he relished it. Not unlike a Chia pet, the only hairless parts of him were the top of his head, the palms of his hands, the bottoms of his feet, and the small ring around his stomach from the fanny pack he wore every day. And no matter what the season, he was a walking heater. When he wasn't wearing his Metro uniform—which he hated because he said the polyester material was too warm and the colors were, as he referred to them, of *excrement colors* because the shirts were yellow and the pants were brown—he wore a tank top and shorts out of which his body hair would spill out like wild ivy. And not unlike Frosty in the Bahamas during the summertime, with any kind of physical activity, he dripped sweat constantly and profusely and, therefore, had to carry napkins to sop them everywhere he went. Even though his personality was somewhat aloof, sarcastic, and intimidating complete with a thunderous voice—even when he wasn't yelling—that could make a cat's hair stand on end, he wouldn't hurt a flea. He would rather have released an insect back to the outdoors than to have killed it.

*   *   *

Mark was lying face down. They carefully rolled him over and, in doing so, observed that he had been shot several times. The firefighters immediately proceeded with rescue measures, giving him oxygen and CPR. Unable to detect a pulse, they worked on his chest with even more dedication but were eventually instructed to stop helping him. His eyes became fixed and pale grey, his respirations slowed, and with one final breath, they heard him whisper "Lis." Despite their best efforts, they were too late.

Defeated and powerless, they pronounced him dead. And with his soul went a part of me, which I will never recover.

All Are Dispatched to the Scene

*H*omicide, domestic violence, tragedy investigators units and their detectives as well as the coroner's office are dispatched to the scene. City engineers and City light are contacted to assess and repair the bridge. Red Cross is contacted to provide shelter for displaced apartment tenants.

News Coverage: Witness Says, "I Heard a Big Bang . . ."

*W*itness: I heard a big bang and a big crash and then the horrific realization of disaster as a Metro bus plunges forty feet off the Aurora Bridge after the driver is shot. The bus careened through a guardrail and landed onto an apartment below. At the scene right now, which is being called a crime scene, we begin our live coverage with a reporter who is live on the Aurora Bridge. An amazing scene, this is what is left of the bus, an amazing and horrific scene of a Metro bus flying off the Aurora Bridge.

Paramedics carried away bloody passengers. Volunteers comforted the injured who were waiting, in stunned silence, to be taken to the hospital. Within two hours of the tragedy, all the injured had been removed and taken to area hospitals.

News Coverage: Look at the Scene Just Moments

*L*ook at the scene just moments after emergency crews showed up—two dozen or more passengers in a variety of conditions some bloody, others on stretchers being carried off, some just dazed. There was a rush to get as many ambulances here as soon as they possibly could. They did a very good job. You can see firefighters scrambling to get some of these people in ambulances and treated as rapidly as possible. People around here found themselves in situations where they had to help. Speaking with witnesses on the ground, many people thought they were going to be hit by falling debris. Incredible stories keep coming in. We'll be back with you with much more later.

* * *

Numb, I sat at my desk, staring at the phone and waiting for Mark's call to reassure me that he was all right, but somehow I knew that the call would never come. I rubbed my eyes. When I opened them, they came to rest on a poster affixed to the wall next to my desk. It read, "Trust in the *Lord* with all your heart and lean not on your own understanding" (Proverbs 3:5). A doctor from the clinic approached me and asked, "Are you all right?" I saw his lips moving, but I didn't hear what he said. I told him that I needed to go home. In a daze, I somehow made it to the bus stop. I sat toward the front as the bus traveled north on I-5. People were straining to see out the west-side windows at the commotion happening across the water on the Aurora Bridge. In my head, a battle was ensuing. One part of my consciousness was telling me it was Mark. The other part was screaming shut up so loudly that I wanted to put my hands over my ears and scream. I wanted to scream for all those people to "sit the hell down and quit staring out the windows!"

* * *

At 1745, Officers Located

At 1745, officers located an AMT Backup .380 pistol near the front door of the bus. More evidence is collected at the scene. Detectives are sent, to each of the hospitals, to interview witnesses and identify the suspect.

News Coverage: Reporter Speaks with the Seattle Police Department

*R*eporter: "Has a weapon been recovered and what can you tell us about the shooter?"

SPD: "We have one weapon recovered. We've been talking to victims on the bus. We want them treated first, but we are trying to determine if we do have the suspect or if that person left the scene before our arrival. We believe the person, who was a passenger on the bus, shot the driver. We do not have specific details as yet. Our officers are trying to get that information from passengers."

*　　*　　*

It seemed to take forever for the bus to reach the park and ride. Finally arriving, I ran to my car. I was on autopilot. I suddenly found myself at home, pulling into my driveway. Jumping out of the car, I ran toward the house. I burst open the door and, immediately, turned on the TV. The battle in my head continued. Trying to convince myself that it wasn't Mark, I repeatedly said out loud, "See, it was the 359 not Mark's 6. He'll be calling soon to tell me so."

*　　*　　*

Firefighters Stood by with a Hose Line

*F*irefighters stood by with a hose line while other firefighters placed several large rescue-lifting bags under the bus. A large heavy-duty Metro tow truck backed up to the wreckage, and together they carefully lifted up the bus. Rescuers checked cautiously underneath for victims, but no additional victims were found.

*　　*　　*

Chapter One: November 27, 1998

The phone rang, startling me out of my self-argument, but my excitement was brief. It was only his sister. Just as upset as I was, she too believed that it wasn't Mark because she also knew that he was to be driving the number 6 that day. As she spoke, I heard a car pull up into our driveway. I looked at the TV again. The news media showed firefighters performing CPR on the driver.

News Coverage: Just After Three This Afternoon

*J*ust after three this afternoon, Metro bus route 359, filled with some two dozen passengers, was headed over the Aurora Bridge when somehow it left the road, falling some forty feet onto an apartment building. Witnesses below each have their own terrifying accounts of the moment the bus left the bridge. Some ran for cover as huge blocks of concrete fell toward them, others could only stare dazed and in disbelief. Police say a passenger on the bus, just before the crash, shot the driver of the bus. Live now, we are below the bridge. You can see the guardrail where the bus went off. We understand a crane will be brought in to extricate what is left from the wreckage of the bus. Police say the suspect is among the injured in all of this. More details of how this all began as information becomes available.

Everything that transpired next seemed to happen in slow motion. I saw a familiar white sedan parked in the driveway. My heart sank. For a brief moment, I had a flashback from my childhood. I remembered city officials in a similar car coming to pick up my sister and me. Reality came back to me like a ton of bricks as I realized why those people were there. The phone slipped from my hands, and I walked slowly toward the door. "He's gone! He's gone! He's gone!" my mind screamed. I pressed my hands over my ears to quiet the noise.

*   *   *

News Pilot: As You Can See the Fremont Area

$\mathscr{A}$s you can see, the Fremont area is very populated. When we arrived on the scene, we saw a number of people rushing to the scene offering their assistance— aid units and fire units. I've lost count of how many aid units have left for area hospitals. Reporting live.

News Coverage: As SPD Stated
This Is a Crime Scene

$\mathscr{A}$s SPD stated this is a crime scene now, standing under the bridge, you can see a large crane has been backed in. They are going to lift the bus to see if anyone is underneath it. Update on injuries, there are fifteen victims in critical condition. This is a massive, massive tragedy, massive, massive response. It will be a long time before all the questions here get answered. Reporting live.

News Coverage: The Smell of Diesel Is in the Air

$\mathscr{T}$he smell of diesel is in the air, a concern they must have while trying to move the bus. The major effort to get the people, who were injured on the bus, to local area hospitals has been accomplished as all the aid units have left the scene. Yet still a number of police and fire units are on the scene, standing by in case there are any problems with the fuel spill as well as securing the scene. It's been confirmed there are no victims underneath the bus, and the fuel spill has been contained. Reporting live.

*   *   *

The car doors opened, and two people climbed out. I opened the door. I yelled at them to go away. My knees felt like jelly. Like Alice in wonderland, I felt myself falling into some nightmarish reality. "No no no!" I screamed over and over again, and then my body crumpled. I felt hands on my elbows, supporting me and stopping my fall. The two people were Mark's supervisors. They told me what I already knew—that something horrible happened and that Mark was dead.

*   *   *

With the attention and efforts of four firefighters, a ladder truck carefully removed Mark's body from the roof. The media recorded its slow descent, etching the scene permanently into the minds of thousands of viewers. On a backboard, secured and far from the media, his body—covered with a yellow rescue blanket and a tarp—laid waiting under the bridge for the coroner.

News Coverage: As Rescuers Tried Unsuccessfully

As rescuers tried unsuccessfully to revive the driver, they realized they had more than a horrible tragedy on their hands—they had a murder. The driver has gunshot wounds. This dramatically has changed the focus of this tragedy. Somewhere, among these wounded people, is the suspect who may still have a weapon on them, adding terror to an already nightmarish scene. Right now, we know at least two people are dead, and at least twenty-seven to thirty people have been hurt in this entire tragedy. Reporting live.

*   *   *

Mark's supervisors said that we had to go to the hospital. I went back to the phone. Incoherently, through tears, I told Mark's sister that Mark's supervisors were there, that Mark was the driver of the bus, and that they were taking me to the hospital. I don't remember hanging up the phone. On the way to the hospital, I babbled and cried incoherently. I don't remember a thing I said.

Elise Crawford

* * *

News Coverage: Reporting Live from Harborview

*R*eporting live from Harborview Medical Center, where the most critical have been taken, hospital spokespeople say the doctors and surgeons in the emergency room are working furiously on the three most critical of the victims. They say the extents of other injuries are broken bones, and there are no burns. Among the critically injured is a victim with a gunshot wound to the head. They aren't saying for sure, but they may have some idea of what may have happened tonight. Reporting live.

* * *

Like a Hollywood movie, the hospital was surrounded by police. There were news crews and cameras everywhere. I was ushered away from them through a side door and into a private waiting area. It was like Grand Central Station. People were everywhere. In the waiting area, King County executives filed in and out, offering me deep-felt words of condolence. Their voices blended together, monotone and garbled. I felt a sea of arms, coming from all directions, to offer me hugs for comfort. I desperately clung on to each person, hording their positive energy and hoping there would be enough to snap me out of this nightmarish dream fog. But my efforts were in vain as I realized that no amount of hugs or energy could bring me back the reality I so desperately sought.

* * *

News Coverage: We're Just Getting Word

*W*e're just getting word into the newsroom, confirmed information, that the suspect in this tragedy—the one who pulled the trigger, shooting the bus driver, forcing him to swerve off the road—is confirmed dead. For those of you expecting loved ones home, who ride the bus over the Aurora Bridge, we will have a phone number for you to call shortly.

*   *   *

My request to be taken to Mark fell on deaf ears. I was continually put off. In frustration, I begged the hospital staff to let me see him. A hospital counselor was called instead. She sat down with me to calmly explain that because this was a homicide investigation, I would not be allowed to see Mark until it was completed. I didn't care what her rationalization was. Through tears and near hysteria, I pleaded with her, "Please, at least allow me to touch his hand so I can be convinced that it's true!" I wanted to touch him as I remembered him, warm, not cold—not dead. She told me she couldn't—that she wasn't allowed to. I cried harder. I couldn't make myself understand her reason. Nothing made sense. I just wanted to be with him. I wanted to see for myself. I wanted proof. I wanted to touch Mark.

Amidst the confusion, my best friend arrived. She took me into her arms, rocked me gently, and soothingly stroked my hair. She led me out of the room and out a back hallway to her car. Her husband drove. She asked if I would like to come home with her. I declined; I wanted to go home. Once at my house, she walked me in and asked again if I would be all right alone. I assured her that I would be and hugged her goodbye.

Exhausted, I prepared for bed. Skipping the Pooh-and-Piglet flannel pajamas Mark gave me for my birthday, I chose a T-shirt of his from the laundry instead and changed for bed. Finding a *fragrant* work shirt of his from the day before, I pulled it over his pillow. Getting into bed, I noticed for the first time that my side of the bed was cold as was his. Shivering, I curled my body around his pillow and buried my face into the smell of his shirt and cried. I prayed and I cried until my throat and eyes stung, "Please don't let this be true. Please, please, Mark, come home." Eventually, beyond exhaustion, I fell into a deep sleep.

Chapter Two: A Love Story

Time in a Bottle

If I could save time in a bottle
The first thing that I'd like to do is to save every day
Till eternity passes away just to spend them with you
If I could make days last forever
If words could make wishes come true
I'd save every day like a treasure and then,
Again, I would spend them with you
But there never seems to be enough time
To do the things you want to do
Once you find them
I've looked around enough to know
That you're the one I want to go through time with
If I had a box just for wishes
And dreams that had never come true
The box would be empty
Except for the memory
Of how they were answered by you
But there never seems to be enough time to do the things you want to do
Once you find them
I've looked around enough to know
That you're the one I want to go through time with

The beginning, 1989

The Beginning

It was 1989. I was barely in my twenties and raising two babies—from two different, failed relationships—alone in a tiny apartment in Bothell, Washington. Slightly more emotionally naive than my peers, I learned the ways of the world—especially parenting—by the seat of my pants. Before I had my children, I'd never held a baby before. The day Dale was placed in my arms and I was told to take him home was the most frightening day of my life. Then shortly after, Lexi came along like a whole other infant. I was always in a chronic state of anxiety for fear of not being a good mother. It took me a long time to feel really comfortable in the role of being a mother. As young as I was—in spite of the overwhelming challenges and responsibilities before me from the day they were born—I made a solemn promise to myself never to give the naysayers in society a reason to doubt my parental abilities. The three of us were one above all else. I had gotten myself into the predicament, and I was determined to make the best of it.

Because I didn't drive, we rode the bus everywhere. This is how we met Mark McLaughlin, Seattle Metro bus driver number 2106. No matter what the day or time was, when we set out for a ride on the bus, he seemed to always be our driver. Unlike other drivers who would keep their foot on the brake and wait impatiently while I struggled to board with my cumbersome load, Mark would put the bus in park and help. Each time was just like the first. As if he had performed this routine a thousand times before, his actions were always synchronized. First, he would assist Dale up the big steps and help him into a seat. Then with a toss into the air, he would take Lex into his big arms, and

49

simultaneously, while he folded the stroller, he would offer me his arm and escort me up the steps as well. Only after we were situated and seated would he continue with his route. He made me feel special. Even though I knew he probably helped others the same way, I still felt special. This is how it was every time we rode on Mark's bus route.

The rides with Mark were entertaining and uneventful. He always had candy for Dale and some, eventually, for Lex as she got older and lots of stories for me—nothing personal, just worldly knowledge. He knew about so many things. When he spoke, it was with purpose. When he didn't have a story to tell, he had little to say. He didn't rattle on randomly about things as I did. Some of his stories were based on his theories of theology. Although Buddhism interested him the most, he spent a lot of time telling me Christian stories from the Bible. Even though I saw myself as more of a spiritual kind of person, ignorant of Christianity, I listened inquisitively and with an open mind. When the time came to leave his bus, I always went away with a message or two of encouragement. To me, he was the smartest and wisest person I had ever known.

As knowledgeable as he was, his sense of humor was his best attribute. He always seemed to know when I needed cheering up because, on those days, he would tell me the funniest stories—usually about animals. His animated expressions and tones of voice always made me laugh sometimes to the point of tears or stomach cramps or both. The more undivided attention and interest I took in his stories, the more he would open up and tell me. His genuine friendship was infectious. We couldn't help to anticipate our next trip with him. If we ever happened to have a different driver, my tiny and usually quiet little boy would release his true two-year-old attributes with full vengeance. With a bright red face and tears pouring from his eyes, he would adamantly refuse to get onto the bus. He wanted only to ride on Mark's bus not with the man presently driving. And what a scene he'd make. My explanation, that it wasn't Mark's turn to drive, would only pacify him temporarily. From then on, whenever we set out for a bus trip, he would keep a vigilant eye open for his favorite driver.

One day, as we were heading home on Mark's bus, he invited us to join him on his break. Because my apartment in Bothell was where his route ended and I felt comfortable enough to be alone with him, I agreed to stay. When we arrived at the end of the line, Mark brought a camera out from his workbag. He said he loved to take pictures of nearly everything and asked permission to take one of the children and me. I felt a little self-conscious as I didn't look my best, but he made me laugh anyway as he clicked the button on the camera—a bittersweet moment caught in time. Dale—a slight, pale-haired two-year-old little boy with big blue eyes—glared into the lens of Mark's camera while Lexi, a brown-eyed chubby two-month old with just a tuft of brown hair on the top of her head, snuggled up inside her carrier that was secured to the front of me. That photo was the very first of many. Before long, the lunchtime visits turned into a weekly ritual.

Ironically, I forgot about that photo until I came across it ten years later. Even stranger, although we were alone with Mark and parked in a secluded neighborhood, there appears to be a mysterious figure in the stairwell of the bus just behind Lexi's head.

Sometimes, during these visits, we would walk a half of a block to the Safeway grocery store, which was just around the corner from where Mark parked his bus during his breaks, and buy lunch. We bought juice and baby food for Lex; finger foods, juice, and crackers for Dale; and deli sandwiches for us. On our way out the store, it became customary to stop at the candy machines to buy a treat and for the children to ride the coin-operated horse. Before we ate our lunch, it was customary for Mark to feed the birds first. He always had birdseed with him and was particular where he fed them. The Bothell and the Sand Point Way locations were his favorite. The birds somehow knew when their favorite driver was coming because—like a scene from an Alfred Hitchcock movie—hundreds of them would appear out of nowhere as soon as he parked his bus. The kids would watch with intense curiosity while he poured a pound of seed, the length of the bus, onto the sidewalk. And as soon as he finished, we'd hurriedly scramble back inside of the bus to watch the birds eat. The kids really got a kick out of this. Their high-pitched, elfish baby giggles were contagious as they echoed and bounced off the walls of the empty bus. When our lunchtime visits came to an end, with all of the seed gone and not a bird in site, Dale would sit on Mark's lap and *drive* us the half block to our apartment.

Seasons in the Sun

*E*ventually, the kids and I moved a few miles down the road to another apartment in Lake City. We got so caught up in the routine of our lives that we soon lost track of Mark. Dale grew into a handsome preschooler, and Lexi blossomed into a beautiful toddler with a head full of bouncy brown curls. In spite of their growth spurts, they continued to hold on to the same infectious laugh that they were born with. Dale attended Head Start, and Lexi attended the campus day-care nursery school where I took classes at a local community college. Our daily schedule was time-consuming mostly because of the ordeal of getting to and from the college each day. After Dale left on the school bus, Lex and I would take a city bus from our apartment south quite a distance so we could catch a bus back north a very long distance to the school and vice versa back home—rain, sleet, or snow. By the time we made it home—with dinner to be made, lunches to be packed, clothes to be laid out for the next day, baths to give, and stories to be read—there was little time for anything else.

One day, as fate would have it and as Lex and I transferred onto our final bus home from the college, we happened to board Mark's bus. As soon as she saw him, she squealed with delight and hurriedly tripped up the giant stairs of the bus and fell right into his lap. She wrapped her little arms around his stomach as far as she could stretch them and hugged him as tightly as she could. His face lit up, and he hugged her in return. He was just as happy to see us again too. I claimed my unofficial seat, the one directly across from his driver's seat, where we could see each other best and where we could talk most privately. I spoke a mile a minute and brought him up to date on the current events in our lives before we reached our intended stop. I only paused long enough to catch my breath or to move if an elderly or disabled person needed my seat, and then I'd quickly reclaim it after they left. Much to my surprise, my scheduled bus trips now coincided with his current bus route, allowing us to visit with him more often.

Eventually, we joined him once again for his lunch breaks. But because we no longer lived in Bothell, it was something we could only do occasionally as this type of trip would consume half of a day. We would have to ride with him south all the way into downtown Seattle, then north out to Bothell to the end of the line for our traditional lunchtime visit, and then south again back to Lake City. During one of our visits with Mark, he noticed a little Barbie doll peeking out of Lexi's carry case. He told her that it reminded him of me and asked her if he could have it. He promised to take very good care of it and that he would bring it to work with him every day. She gladly gave it to him. If he asked for all of her toys, she would have willingly surrendered them all. This is how I acquired the nickname Dollface.

That doll became yet another one of Mark's controversial acts of defiance, both on the bus and back at his bus base, mostly because he undressed it and had its boobs hanging out over the side of his workbag for all to see. Despite the stir it caused, he never put it away. He claimed that he had even been offered money for it. Even so, after several years and several hundred bus rides later—as disgustingly filthy and an eyesore it became—he would never part with it. Other than the doll, Mark loved to share. He would give you the shirt off his back if he thought you needed it. So you can just imagine how difficult it was for him to restrain his innate instinct to *help* me. Although he never could comprehend the delicate sense of pride I had for myself and my circumstances, he respected my boundaries and never judged me just the same. Inconspicuously though, overtime, he convinced me that his acts of kindness were expressions of *just sharing* not helping. Like the occasional clothes he brought for Dale, which his son—who was three years older—had outgrown, or the times that he *happened* to be going by my place whenever Lex and I were leaving for the college with the lure of apple fritters and coffee to be had along the way.

Surrender

*T*ime continued to evolve, and so did Mark's feelings for me. When the gradual changes in his demeanor became more apparent, I began to feel uncomfortable around him. I regarded him as a friend and nothing more. Not only was he was eleven years my senior and a foot and three inches taller, but he also outweighed me by nearly two hundred pounds. No, he definitely was not boyfriend material for me. Besides, I had worked too hard and come too far and was not interested in repeating history. To make my point without hurting his feelings, I explained, as gently as I could, that I wasn't attracted to him other than just being his friend. I made the excuse that I didn't want to be the *other woman*. That I knew, from experience, how it felt to be the one cheated on. And most importantly, I didn't want to be a midlife crisis for him. I suggested that we not see each other outside of his work anymore. He was disappointed and devastated. It was evident in his eyes. Hurting his feelings hurt me too.

He kept his distance reluctantly but continued to call regularly to check on us, to see how we were doing. Continually challenged with seemingly insurmountable conditions set by the government, the children and I were forced to move yet again. I hated uprooting the kids. I was always zigzagging my way through the county, hoping that the next place we landed would be longer than six months. In spite of the hassle, I was happy with the apartment I found for us. It was located across the street from my mother's apartment and walking distance to the grocery store, the bus stop, the YMCA day care, and the post office. During a phone conversation with Mark, I shared that we had to move again. He insisted that he be allowed to help. Because his strength would make the move faster and easier, I gladly invited him. When the work was finished and while we rested with a cold soda, he asked me casually if I had ever been to Whidbey Island. Before I had a chance to answer that I hadn't, he asked me if I would I like to join him for a day trip. Against my better judgment, but enticed by the chance to get away for a while, I agreed to go.

And I'm glad I did. I had a wonderful time. He was the perfect tour guide, historian, and gentleman as always. While we strolled on the beach, he wove a tale about the island's intriguing military past. While I listened, I searched intensely for pretty seashells. My favorite was the ever-elusive, multicolored hermit shell, but I could only find broken ones. Without missing a beat of his conversation, with hardly any effort at all, the most perfect shells would magically appear to him; and he'd offer them to me. By the time we walked the length of the beach and back, our pockets were stuffed with smelly, sandy seashells. When we left the beach, the sun had begun its descent. On our way back to the ferry, we decided to stop at one of his favorite restaurants for a bite to eat.

Chapter Two: A Love Story

It was a quaint little place with a large windmill, on the outside, near the entrance. I had never been to a nicer restaurant. I felt a little nervous and out of place especially since we smelled like beachcombers and were a little windblown. But thankfully, we fit in with everyone else. We sat at a cozy little table next to a fireplace. We laughed and joked throughout our dinner mostly because of how he demonstrated fancy restaurant etiquette with the *proper* use of the napkin and eating utensils. After dinner, while we waited for our dessert—baked Alaska—and coffee, he became unusually quiet. His eyes sparkled from the firelight as he looked at me. His gentle brown eyes seemed different. I took a deep breath. It caught in my throat. He seemed to see right through my very soul. He reached under the table for my hand. Transfixed by his piercing gaze, I willingly surrendered it to him. The warm and cozy fireplace suddenly became overwhelmingly hot. It was unbearable. I thought I was going to die.

My blouse stuck to my skin. I thought I would dissolve into my chair any moment. I had to remind myself to breath. It was all I could do to remain seated and not run screaming out of the restaurant. I searched his eyes for answers. The imperfections I once saw melted away. He was perfect—this handsome gentle giant. I thought my heart would leap out of my chest. At that very moment, I realized how much I loved him, how I had always loved him. I watched helplessly as my theories about men and relationships in general intertwined with the smoke from the fire and dissipated up the chimney and into thin air. I think he saw the change in my eyes because he smiled reassuringly. He said that he loved me more than life itself and that he wasn't about to lose me. It was exactly the way I felt about him.

I looked away from his eyes, interrupting the spell that we both were under. Tears welled up in my eyes, and my voice quivered as I explained once more that I didn't want to be an affair for him nor a midlife crisis. Squeezing my hand reassuringly, he said that I meant much more to him than that. With my wits about me once again, during the drive back to the ferry, I agreed to date him but only after he had met certain criteria. First and foremost, he'd have to move from the house that he shared with his wife; secondly, he'd have to remove his wedding ring. And lastly, he'd have to file for divorce. My ultimatums didn't discourage him nor did they put a damper on the rest of the evening. From that day forward, we were like two kids that finally got what they've always wanted for Christmas.

Time in a Bottle

*L*exi's fourth birthday was fast approaching. She had sprouted into a willowy preschooler with a head full of beautiful shoulder-length, naturally curly auburn hair with only a hint of baby chubbiness remaining in the apples of her cheeks. I no sooner had put her and Dale to bed when Mark showed up at my door. He held up a piece of paper in his left hand with a noticeable white line on his left ring finger, and—with a devilish grin a mile wide—he asked, "Now?" Surprised and speechless, I laughed and nodded as I jumped into his arms. He picked me up, wrapped his big powerful arms around me, and kissed me. I was so happy that I cried. It was hard to believe that someone could love me so much. I hugged him as tightly as I could and whispered over and over again, into his ear, how much I loved him.

Now a couple, Mark seemed hell-bent to prove that he was not like the other men I had known in the past. Soon after we began dating, he took it upon himself to assure that the children and I were happy and that we had everything we needed. If something was broken, he fixed it. If there was a problem, he helped to solve it. If there were transportation needs, he was right there. If he thought we were starving, well, I believe he thought we were always starving because he was always offering us food either by taking us to a restaurant, buying groceries, or giving us treats. He enjoyed introducing new foods to us that we were not accustomed to eating—mostly because they were not the types of foods available at the local grocery store. Eventually, I had to put limits on how much I would let him help. Not meaning to be stubborn, I explained, as gently as I could, that what I needed most was his love and support not his monetary help. In silent agreement, he led me to believe that he respected my wishes. Over time though, unaware of his contradiction, he slowly and unsuspectingly whittled away at my independent nature until I didn't realize how much I hadn't been doing things for myself anymore.

Chapter Two: A Love Story

We continued to visit Mark on the bus. His shifts always began and ended at his home base, the North Base. Occasionally, he would bring the children and I there to visit. The children's favorite thing to do at the base—besides running helter-skelter in the hallways and around the driver's lockers—was to play in the break room with the pool table and the pinball machines. The best time they had was the year that Mark brought them to visit South Base when Metro had a Halloween party with a haunted house at the southern entrance of the underground bus tunnels. Mark never grew tired of being with us. After we began dating, he went out of his way to assure at least one of his bus routes passed by my apartment to make it easier for us to visit with him. One route, in particular, happened to end close by my place. So when we could, we would visit him for a nostalgic trip to the closest store for lunch, candy, and junk food. If we rode into town with him, we'd either stop at South Base to visit with some of his fellow bus buddies or we'd stop by the International District for a great big bag of homemade fortune cookies and a huge portion of barbecued pork from one of the local vendors. And as if we weren't full already, he would take us out for dinner before he brought us home.

He usually took us to the Armadillo in Woodinville or Ivar's in Fremont. We could only visit Ivar's on nice days because we preferred to eat in the outside dining area. We loved to watch the Fremont Bridge open and close for the passing boats and to feed the seagulls and little birds our French fries. It was as if they were circus trained with the way they performed hilarious antics in hopes of coaxing more fries from us. It was inevitable, whenever I least expected it, that a gull would unsuspectingly snatch a fry from my fingers and make me scream and laugh myself silly. It was moments like these, when I seemed the most happiest, that Mark seemed the most happiest too. It was evident in the way that his eyes lit up like his favorite star on top of the Bon Marche at Christmas time.

Sometimes, when Mark had the day off from work, he took the children and I on minioutings mostly to visit his favorite Seattle haunts. The first place he took us to was to see an enormous statue of a troll that sits underneath the Aurora Bridge. I thought it was rather intimidating and foreboding in a creepy sort of way, but the kids loved it. He sat Lex on its lap while Dale explored all around it. I watched and observed as they roared with laughter. While he played with them, their little faces radiated with happiness. No one would have ever guessed that he wasn't their natural father. He was so patient and kind with them. I didn't think it was possible to love him anymore than I already did, but watching him that day confirmed it tenfold. He took us to visit other places too like the Pike Place Market, the Piers, the Ballard Locks, Discovery Park, and ferry rides to nowhere in particular just to name a few. Though these places might seem commonplace to any other family, to the children of a single mother who didn't drive, each new place was like visiting Disneyland all over again.

Once a year, he took us to a little carnival that was held at a church or parochial school where he spent most of his younger years. There were always tons of fun activities for the kids to do—face painting, games for prizes, minirides, and more. And while the kids played, Mark and I would browse around and enjoy all the handcrafted items that were for sale. As usual, he told me of the history of the church and the story behind a plaque displayed in one of the hallways. It is a dedication in his father's memory.

Eventually, he took us to meet his mother. She welcomed us with open arms. She took to me almost immediately. Over time, we referred to each other endearingly as Lucy and Ethel. She and I were Mark's best girls. It was customary for his mom to receive flowers whenever Mark brought some for me. The kids and I loved to visit her. No matter what the day or time was, she always prepared food for her guests—she never wanted anyone to go home on an empty stomach. Her house was always full of family. People dropped in unannounced at all hours just to visit, and it never bothered her in the least. The holidays were even more fun. Her grandchildren were the center of these events and, gradually, my children were too. Her home was your home. Warmth and laughter could always be found within the walls of her picturesque home.

Yin and Yang

As our new relationship unfolded, I gradually relaxed and let my guard down. I let myself fall head-over-heels and blindly in love with

Chapter Two: A Love Story

Mark. I proudly exposed my heart on my sleeve. He was everything I had ever hoped for and everything I believed that didn't exist. He made me aware of my sense of self and accomplishments. In his eyes, I saw my potential, and that made me work even harder. Mark was the opposite. I never understood why he kept his heart so guarded. He was just as aloof romantically as he was personally. It was difficult for him to say the words *I love you*; rather, he would say "remember who loves you." And as equally difficult was his ability to show affection. More often than not—whenever I'd reach up to hug him—he'd stand as tall as he could so I couldn't reach around his neck. This forced me to hug him around his stomach, which I could only reach partway around. And rather than hug me in return, he'd pat me gently, yet passively, on my shoulders. It was hard not to take his lack of affection personally, and neither a hissy fit nor standing on my head had ever got me any closer to him. He'd just calmly stand by without a word and wait for the storm to pass.

It didn't matter; he remained the same—no public displays of affection other than holding hands. I eventually relented and accepted his terms. And hold his hand I did. I held on to it whenever we were together everywhere and anywhere: while taking walks, watching TV, in the car, or while falling asleep. And Lex did too. For whichever hand was free, his pinky was always reserved for her. I gradually learned to accept his way of showing affection. His gestures and actions spoke louder than any words ever could. I was always aware of his love for me like the many unforgettable visits he secretly made to my apartment when I wasn't home. He would leave little surprises for me to find: a box of decadent gourmet candy on the kitchen counter, a surprise gift, or a fragrant bouquet of flowers in the fridge. And occasionally—as was his sense of humor—he'd leave behind a bottle of Pamprin too.

As sure as rain falls in Seattle, the surprises never stopped. And neither did the daily phone calls. Although we didn't have cell phones back then, Mark would find a way to call me. He would call me in the mornings—either from his house or from the bus base—to wish me a good day. And at lunchtime—at either a rest stop or a store—to tell me how his day was going, to see how mine was, and to tell me that he missed me. And lastly, he'd call me at the end of the night to wish me sweet dreams and to say, "Remember who loves you." But most importantly, if there was ever an accident that involved a Metro bus or a driver, he'd pull his bus over at the nearest phone booth and call me. He said that the passengers didn't seem too mind much. But I'm certain that of all them, there were at least a few who made up some of the complaints that waited for him back at the bus base. Eventually, I anticipated his calls and found my days and nights incomplete without them.

Above all, Mark and I were best friends first and always. We could confide our deepest thoughts, dreams, or concerns with each other without judgment or criticism from the other. We were a private couple content to just having each other and our children as the center of our universe. As we evolved, we adopted pet names for each other. First and foremost, we were Hunny Bunny and Dollface. He accepted the endearment I knighted him with as if it were a royal title. He never asked me not to call him with it in public or in front of the children, family, or friends; and so, it was all I ever called him thereafter. I'll never forget the perplexed look on my friend's face the first time she heard me refer to him by that name. She frowned, sized him up and down, and exclaimed, "Hunny Bunny? No, Hunny Sasquatch is more like it!" The way she said it and the expression on her face was so funny that it made me laugh until tears streamed down my face. Yes, I had to agree; Hunny Bunny was an odd endearment for such a big and burly man.

And if we weren't being silly already, we had yet another set of names for each other. Because the size difference between Winnie the Pooh and Piglet and the special friendship they shared was ironically parallel to the differences and the friendship between Mark and me, we referred to each other by these characters names as well. He always said the "Winnie the Pooh and Piglet" idea was my thing, yet he was the always the one buying me Pooh and Piglet memorabilia. One of my favorite gifts, which he gave me, was a framed poster of Pooh and Piglet holding hands and walking into the sunset. It was titled *It's So Much Friendlier with Two*.

Traditions

*I*ntroducing each other's children into our fairy tale was challenging to say the least. The odds were against me, with his children, from

Chapter Two: A Love Story

the beginning. According to them, I would always be the reason for the division of their family, and nothing I did would ever change that. The fact that I was closer to his eldest child's age than I was to Mark's and that I lacked the experience of parenting maturity didn't help matters much either. Holidays, however, melted the ice for the most part. So Mark and I made a concerted effort to make them as fun as we could. As the holidays approached, Mark would get the kids pumped up for the festivities by getting as excited as they were. To say it was chaotic is putting it mildly. I looked forward to the brief period in between the fervor and the next one.

Each year, as Easter rolled around, Mark would take the "decorating of the eggs" ritual very seriously. He even had a special kitchen drawer, just for his decorating arsenal, stocked with the latest and greatest decorating tools. He would show the children how to make—without breaking them—"really cool eggs." Even though his eggs outshined all of theirs, they never seemed to notice; he had a special way of making them feel as if theirs were just as much of a masterpiece as were his own. Because he liked to decorate a lot of eggs and hated the thought of having tons of hard-boiled eggs to be eaten up, he chose to color them fresh from the carton. They never had a chance to spoil because they were gobbled up on our next customary Sunday breakfast—green egg and ham omelets rolled into warmed flour tortillas.

Christmas time was equally fun. No sooner had I taken a batch of sugar cookies out of the oven and placed them on the table, Mark would be the first to snatch some up, to stockpile the ones he wanted to decorate. I love the pictures of the first year we decorated Christmas cookies together. My favorite is of Dale sitting on his knees, working alongside Mark, while Lex sat next to them, struggling to shake a bottle of decorations in her chubby little hands. But Mark didn't stop there. He also decorated the inside and outside of the house especially the Christmas tree. He wouldn't settle for an ordinary tree bought from a street-side vendor, the kind my children and I were used to. Rather, he would bundle up like a lumberjack; and with his antique mitered handsaw at the ready, he'd pick and cut down a fresh one from a local tree farmer, an older man that Mark admired. And once he had his prized tree, he would give the farmer and his wife a freshly baked Marionberry pie—his favorite—from the local Gai's Bakery and yummy treats for their dogs as a thank-you gift. Oddly enough, the farmer's dogs somehow remembered him. The next year Mark came for a tree, they'd instantly recognize his truck and rush out to greet him.

Then there were birthdays. Mark went to great lengths to make the day special for whoever's birthday it was. So in return, I made sure that his birthdays were also just as special. His fortieth birthday was particularly memorable. With his mom and his sister's help, we decorated his house and put out his favorite cake—angel food with strawberries and whipped cream. He was sure surprised when he arrived home, from work, that day. The pictures of his beaming face say it all. That year, the children were as particularly anxious for him to open his gifts as they were to have some of his birthday cake. It wasn't the pewter key chain, in the shape of an angel with the words *Drive Safe* inscribed on it, that excited them. It was the personal cross-stitched biography we made together they were most eager to give him.

It took several months, and the children helped to create it. First, I stitched the colors of his heritage—Irish and Ukraine—on cross-stitch cloth to make a border. Second, inside of the heritage border in yet another border format, I stitched—following the patterns from graphing paper that the children drew—objects and symbols that represented Mark the most. And for the final touch, I stitched a poem that I wrote in the center of it. Because it was meant to be a surprise, it had to be hidden throughout its creation. As a result, it is permanently creased down the center from being folded and refolded so many times. When it was finished, I had it professionally framed. The crease is barely noticeable. It turned out perfectly, especially with the nonglare glass and the mahogany wood that surrounds it. The children were as proud as they could be and beside themselves the day we gave it to him. It was the biggest secret they had ever kept, and for that, he loved it all the more. He proudly displayed it on his living room wall for all to see.

For Father's Day one year, I had the children create a different kind of button for him to wear to work. Each chose a picture of themselves that they liked the most and cut it down to size, glued the pictures onto a circle of yellow construction paper, and by consensus, had me write the words *We love you, Daddy* for the heading. I had it professionally laminated and put into a button cover. He was surprised the day he opened it. He wore it proudly that day and for every Father's Day thereafter.

As our families blended together, we created more nontraditional rituals. Like a reincarnated Peter Pan, Mark's childish nature would emerge without warning and infect our children as well. It didn't do a bit of good to scold him and tell him to act his age because he would inevitably make me laugh. And my laughter was all the permission he needed to continue with his antics especially if he had a captive audience. At heart, he was just as much of a kid as they were so it was easy for him to relate to them. Sometimes I felt as if I had five kids, instead of our blended four, especially when he commenced the ritualistic fart on top of the boys' heads. The best time to perform this was when they were lying on the living room floor and distracted with a movie or a video game. And before they could comprehend what was about to happen, he'd sneak up on them, bend, and let out a big and gassy fart on top of their heads. Although grossed out, they'd laugh every time he got them until their sides hurt. This, in turn—after such a heartwarming display of affection—would start a chain reaction of chaos, disorder, and lewd and outlandish behavior. I was definitely outnumbered in any attempt to regain order after one of those incidents.

And then there were rituals that belonged to Mark and Lexi alone like the way he picked her up. From the very first time he carried her up the steps of the bus, he'd reach down, swoop her up into the air, and then rub noses with her before setting her down again. Even to this day, Lexi has a photo of one of those moments hung above her bed just before she was too big to be picked up anymore. And then there was the way he tucked her into bed at night. After tucking the blankets securely underneath her chin, he'd gently plant a kiss on her little forehead and wish her sweet dreams. The boys, however, would get a "go to sleep" just before he closed their door for the night. From the very first time he held her as a baby, he had a special place in his heart for her. She could talk a mile in a minute and repeat the most outlandish and repetitive knock-knock jokes ever heard. As if he had never heard them before, he would patiently give her his undivided attention and laugh at each and every one. Even though he had three boys to roughhouse with and even though she could be just as rambunctious as they were and even though she could be the most trying of them all, Lexi still was his precious little girl. She could get away with things that none of the boys ever could. And he always made special time just for her without the *annoying* boys or Mom. No matter if they went to feed the ducks or just run errands, their time alone was sacred.

A Proposal

Our relationship continued to revolve around his bus routes. Like the day he asked me to marry him—well, you know Mark—the day he indirectly asked me to marry him. One summer day, while I was visiting him for a customary end-of-the-route lunch, I put my hands out to catch something that he tossed to me, which wasn't unusual as he always tossed treats to me in this manner. But that day was different. What I caught wasn't Godiva chocolates. What I caught was a miniature perfectly square baby blue box with a tiny yellow bow on top of it.

I looked to him for an explanation, but he continued to drive as if nothing out of the ordinary just happened. I chose not to open the little package until we got to the end of the line, which seemed to be a million miles away. As we drove, every nerve in my body seemed to twitch. I held the tiny box tightly in my hands and mixed emotions ran amuck in my head in anticipation of what was inside. When we finally reached Bothell, he parked the bus in the usual place and nonchalantly stood up and stretched. He stopped midway when he noticed that I hadn't opened the box yet. "Well?" he asked, "aren't you going to open it?" He knelt next to my seat as I gingerly opened the delicate box. Inside, I found yet another small box—a black velvet one. My hands shook as I opened it. As if opening a long-lost treasure chest, when the light found the stone within, a kaleidoscope of colors burst throughout the interior of the bus, shimmering and sparkling like hundreds of little fireflies. It reflected off my face and made the walls of the entire bus glitter. It was the most beautiful ring I ever saw. I was speechless. I had never been given a ring before. He explained that he had chosen the stone because it was the same hypnotic blue as my eyes, and the band was the same gold as my hair.

Just as nervous as I was, he carefully removed the ring from the box and gently placed it on my left ring finger. It fit perfectly. "Well?" he asked, expecting me to answer a question that he hadn't asked. Still speechless, tears flowed down the apples of my cheeks in little rivers. In a futile war with my mascara, I carefully wiped the tears away and mumbled incoherently an indirect answer to his indirect question. In so many words, I explained that before I would accept, I wanted to become self-sufficient. I wanted to finish school, to learn to drive, and to have my first professional job. Our eyes met. I could see my reflection within them. I saw who he knew I was. I saw my potential and the high regard he had for my success. And I saw that he was already contemplating how he was going to help me accomplish the goals I set for myself. My ultimatums did not faze him in the past nor did they then. For the moment, the best I could do was to give him my commitment that someday I would be ready. And then I really began to cry. I cried because of how safe and loved he made me feel for the first time in my life and because I was afraid that I loved him too much. He gathered me into his big strong arms and caressed my hair consolingly, knowing that holding me this way made me forget about whatever had upset me. Holding me even closer, he whispered lovingly into my ear that he understood and that he would wait for as long as I needed, and then he gently kissed my tears away ever so sweetly. I nodded and hugged him tightly in return. Even so, my consciousness remained unconvinced to raise the white flag so quickly.

With the blindness of a love-struck teenager, I laughed at the reality of it all and wrapped my arms around his neck. While we ate our lunch, we daydreamed aloud about our future. Like the weaving of a spider's web, the more we planned, the further it stretched out before us. Mark wanted the Armadillo restaurant to cater our wedding. Imagining him and the guests in formal attire, trying not to get BBQ sauce on their clothes as they ate, made me laugh; it was just like him. There wasn't a day that I didn't catch myself daydreaming into the deep blue stone. It seemed to go on forever like my future. I wasn't just surviving anymore; life now had meaning, and I smiled with a seemingly permanent Cheshire grin. In the following days, we had our *official* engagement pictures taken.

Family Time

*A*fter our engagement, we spent even more time together primarily on weekends and holidays because of our busy schedules. The weekdays seemed to go by slowly before we were reunited again. Our brief seventy-two-hour visits flew by because Mark planned them to the very second. He made sure that none of our precious time was wasted. Saturdays were usually reserved for an outing—no sleeping in. And Sundays were spent running errands, which were just as fun as the Saturday outings. Though we were always on the go, he was creative in how he divided his time between us. None of us ever felt neglected or less loved.

Because he cherished the great outdoors—the windier and colder, the better—his first activity of choice was to head to the beach. On the days I thought it was too cold for an outside adventure, I would exclude myself by exaggerating how much homework I had to do. Without a second thought, he would gladly pack up all of the children and disappear almost an entire day. More often than not, I would find myself catching up on some much-needed time alone with a cup of coffee and a good book or some much-needed sleep. If the beach wasn't in the plans, he would plan a new place for us to hike. And just as serious as the "decorating of the eggs" ritual, the "planning of the hike" ritual required just as much calculating preparation. He found ideas for hikes and family treks in the Sunday paper. He only kept the ones that he thought we might enjoy the best and saved them in a special file. We rarely went on the same hike twice.

Chapter Two: A Love Story

He went to great lengths to prepare for a hike. First, he prepared a backpack so full of all the things he thought we required—a picnic feast, a camera and extra film, a first aid kit, water, rain gear, and clothes and shoes appropriate for hiking—that he was the only one able to carry it. Next, he double-checked that the children and I were dressed and prepared for the type of outing we were going on. And finally, of course, he brought food for the animals. I enjoyed the hikes in the fall best. The scenic country roads were breathtaking, and the trees were beautiful in the way they hung over the entire road with their multicolored shades of red, gold, and orange leaves. The trails for the hikes were usually off the main highway and all the way to the end of the side roads.

Mostly rugged, it was the children's favorite part of the drive because Mark, much to my protest, would throw all of his professional driving habits over the cliffs and make what the children called fishtails and 360s until we reached the start of the trail. I swear we were close to going over a couple of times. The more I protested, screeched, and made horrifying faces, the faster and riskier he would drive—all the while laughing like some wild, crazy man, encouraging the children to laugh and holler along with him, and jangling my nerves to no end. But somehow, we always made it safely to our hiking destination. I don't know if this was his twisted way of getting the kids ready for a hike, but it always seemed to work. They were pumped with enough adrenaline to last them for the entire hike. There was never a complaint of being tired or bored not even from little Lexi. In fact, I was usually the one pulling up the rear.

The hikes were just as magical as were the holidays. We saw the world through Mark's eyes, and it was beautiful. He was our great teacher, a mentor—a Merlin of sorts. With every outing we ventured upon, the children and I gained more appreciation and understanding of human nature, animals, ecology, and religion. I learned more from him than I ever did in school. He taught us about nature, history, and animals. He talked about the different types of trees and how to tell their ages, about plants—the kinds we could eat and touch and the ones we couldn't—and so much more. The hikes were not only unique and exhausting—even if we had been on the same one before—but always educational and fun. So much, in fact, that we would forget about everything else—that is, everything except for the yummy picnic we knew Mark carried in his backpack. As a rule, the partaking of the picnic would not commence until we had made it to the lake or river, our destination for that day. After the picnic, with full stomachs and tired legs, and while we walked at a leisurely pace back to the truck, Mark would toss birdseed into the bushes for his feathered friends. Driving back was always a peaceful treat because the children usually slept until we arrived home.

There is one particular hike I will always remember. One time, rather than tossing the birdseed into the bushes as he usually did, he chose to feed them in the open. To get a closer look, I inched closer to the cute little creatures and then suddenly found myself in the middle of a ritualistic dance. The birds swooped and flew in and out between my legs and all around me in one feathered blur. Simultaneously, they dive-bombed to the ground to scoop up the food Mark threw out for them. In mesmerized disbelief, Mark, the children, and I laughed until our sides ached. It was an indescribable experience. The birds were so trusting, as was any animal that Mark beckoned from the bracken and woods.

In addition to hikes, we spent a lot of family time visiting his favorite place—Whidbey Island. Like the hikes, there was always something new to learn. He took us to every fort, beach, and picnic place on that island. So many, in fact, that I can't distinguish one from the other in the photos I have. Mark's favorite was the lighthouse at Fort Ebey. My favorite place was the Captain's beach house at Fort Casey. I deemed it my dream house. We spent hours exploring the island's beaches. Because the children liked to run ahead, Mark would wager a bet to keep them closer to us. He'd tell them that he would give five dollars to the first one who found a pure white rock. It had to be absent of any markings, and it had to be larger than a quarter, but if he found it first, the bet was off. And it worked like magic. The children remained close to us in hopes of being the first one to find that ever-elusive rock before he did.

Chapter Two: A Love Story

The best and last beach walk we took was to Birch Bay just before the Canadian border. Mark rented a two-bedroom condominium just off the main drag and within walking distance to the beach. It was furnished with many amenities. This was his way—it had to be a four-star place whenever we stayed overnight anywhere. He never explained why. I tried to reason with him that a cost-efficient vacation would make me just as happy. But giving us the best of everything made him happiest. The morning after our arrival, while the children were still sleeping, we decided to take a short walk to the café for my morning latte. The wind was still, the air was warm, and the water lapped lazily close to the sidewalk as the tide hadn't gone out yet. It was the perfect setting for a history lesson. He recounted his own memories of summers past entwined with the area's history.

We stopped briefly to appreciate a majestic bald-headed eagle sitting on top of a phone pole directly above us. Mark said that it had been following us since we left the condo. In awe, we stared at the massive creature a little longer and then continued on our quest for my coffee. With coffee in hand, we headed back to the condo. To our surprise, the eagle had been waiting for us and followed us all the way back to the

Dale waiting for Mark's bus to go by
Bothell, 1989

First Christmas cookie decorating
together, 1993

One of many trips to Whidbey Island

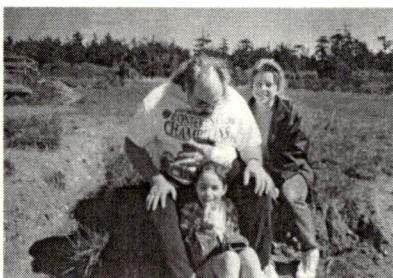

A Love like no other

Engagement photos, 1993

Mark's fortieth birthday, 1994

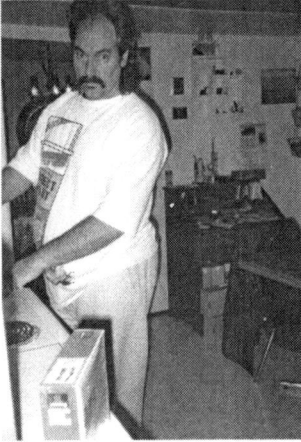

The official weekly preparation of green eggs and ham   *Daddy's girl*

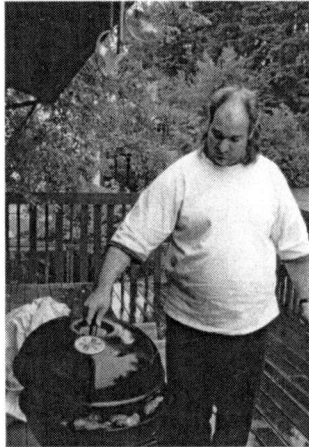

Rain, sleet, or snow, it was always a good time for BBQ

Graduation, Driver's License,   1998   *Mark's first brand new vehicle*
Brand New Car, OH MY !!!!

Our last hike,   1998   *Our last trip to the beach, Birch*
Bay, WA

My birthday trip to Canada, weekend of November 11, 1998

Where we stayed—the Weston Hotel and the saltine cracker skeet-shooter gulls

A promise made

condo, hopping effortlessly from phone pole to phone pole. The eagle's odd behavior opened another dialogue for Mark. He shared his theory of animal spirituality and their relationship with God and with us. Once at the condo, we woke the children for a day at the beach. By the time we went back outside, our guardian eagle was gone but not forgotten.

We set out for the beach armed and ready: sun lotion applied, shorts and tank tops on, sunglasses, beach moccasins, towels, and of course, the camera. To our disappointment, we couldn't see the tide. It was out—way out. It was so far away that we couldn't see the waves on the shore anymore. Undaunted, we set out for the shoreline. The sand was dotted with little puddles and lakes of water. Although I did my best to walk around them, it was futile. Little clam squirts, in between the puddles, made my feet wet no matter what I did. Mark suggested that I remove the moccasins and try walking barefoot. I removed the shoes cautiously and stepped onto the sand. It was as smooth as silk, and the water was warm. The seaweed was slimy and tickly as were the tiny fishes that swam about my toes and feet. The clam squirts surprised me each time they hit my legs. My inner child emerged—which seemed to happen a lot since I had been with Mark—and I burst into a fit of laughter. I swear I never have laughed so hard in my life, which in turn made Mark laugh too. This set the mood for the rest of that wonderful weekend.

Independence

*A*s promised, Mark supported me in my goals toward independence. When I had evening classes, he would drive me to and from the college, care for my children, and bring me dinner on my breaks. Occasionally, if his schedule allowed it, he'd drive me to and from my day classes as well. With his support and the time he made available to edit and proofread my assignments, I managed to complete twenty credits a quarter, work at the college part-time—teaching English writing skills to ESL students—and maintain a 4.0 GPA. He cheered me on all the way.

But our relationship wasn't always a fairy tale. Like every couple, we had our tests and trials. Because of the stress from my school schedule, I created some crazy accusations and started some nasty arguments too. The most difficult issues we faced were the challenges surrounding his new divorce and the creation of our blended family. I had no idea how to deal with all of it. I just wanted the happy ever after. It wasn't long before I began to feel extremely overwhelmed by the pressures and told Mark that I needed to take a break. Although disappointed, he agreed to let me have whatever time I needed to sort things out. During our brief separation, I was continually informed how lost Mark seemed and that his cheerful disposition at work was at an all-time low. Even so, I went on to date other people. But only Mark could fill my empty void, and so I decided to give it another go. We reconciled gradually, and as if the break had never happened, he continued with his quest to help me meet my goals. And before we knew it, it was New Year's Eve again. As we rang in the New Year of 1998, we made a vow that this year would be our best year yet. Shortly after, Mark—true to his word—purchased a house in Lynnwood. It was a very small single-story rambler. I wanted to be excited. I knew he had us as a family in mind, but I couldn't help to wonder how all six of us were going to live peacefully under its small roof. As if he had read my mind, he had a contractor come out to help redesign the house. But no matter how we looked at the floor plans, either up or sideways, none of them passed the zoning requirements. I didn't understand the logistics, but with the goal of adding another member to our family in the near future, there was no other choice than to plan for a bigger house.

That summer, goal number 1 was met. With the love, patience, guidance, and support from the Seattle Milk Fund, I finally graduated from college. We celebrated with the children and my family, and then I immediately began to work on goal number 2—driving lessons. With money from my savings, I had just enough to pay a local driving school, Kirshner, for five lessons plus the driving test. With determination and bullheadedness, I plowed through the lessons. I was nervous on the day of the test but ready. I had made it three-fourths of the way through the test without being docked any points and was in the process of making a left-hand turn across oncoming traffic when an oncoming Metro van hesitated. So I hesitated too and waited for it to pass. As it slowly passed by, the driver—smiling ear to ear—put his head out the window, waved excitedly, and gave me the peace sign. It was Mark. I was docked three points. I had no idea that he would be driving a van and not a bus that day or that he would be driving in the same area of my test. I learned later that he arranged to drive that specific route in coordination with what he believed was the conclusion of my driving test. Regardless of how confined or uncomfortable he was in that little Metro van, he just wanted to show me how proud he was. Perfect score or not, I did it—I got my license! Later that evening, I celebrated my victory with my children and my very own one-man cheering squad.

The following weekend, with license in hand and the rest of my savings, we went to a car tent sale held at Northgate. Because Mark grew up with and was friends with some of the salesmen from Chuck Olson Chevrolet, we didn't have any of the usual hassles. With their kind and entertaining assistance, I found my first car—a little four-door cayenne pepper red Chevy Cavalier. The children begged excitedly to be allowed to ride along for its maiden voyage. The thought of driving by myself with children for the first time made me a nervous wreck. Mark was the first one to get into the car, or so he attempted. I couldn't help but laugh as he struggled to fit into the driver's seat that didn't go back far enough and fight with a steering wheel that wouldn't move. It was the moment when it was time to drive off the lot that I really panicked. Mark pulled his truck out in front of me to follow him and then, assuming I was behind him, took off. It was raining. I couldn't see through the windshield. I didn't know where the levers were for the wipers or how to turn them on. We forgot to go over those minor details. Frantically, *while* I was driving—like Lucy in the chocolate factory—I eventually figured it all out. My kids were beside themselves with laughter; but they were excited, saying, "Yeah! No more bussing it!" His kids thought my driving was hilarious—the way I counted at every stop sign and the way I overcautiously looked both ways several times before I turned—real funny. But thanks to them, I was eventually able to relax. That is, until Mark turned away from the direction of my apartment. Rather than going straight home, he had me follow him to his mom's house to show her what I just bought. By the time we made it back to my apartment, I was high on adrenaline and a sweaty mess.

Chapter Two: A Love Story

To this day, there remains one skill that I will never quite master—parking. Likewise, it took me forever not to be afraid of the gas pump. It scared me to death. I was certain that the fumes would catch fire, and we would all be burned alive. Thankfully though, Mark usually volunteered to put the gas in it. Along with his own vehicle, he made sure that mine not only had gas in it, but also that it was clean and always in working condition. He even changed the tires twice. I swear those tires were nail magnets. And for his peace of mind—I think he was more nervous about me driving than I was—he put a Bible, a first-aid kit, a gallon of water, and a blanket in the trunk of my car; and for extra assurance, he hung a crystal angel from the rearview mirror. Shortly after the arrival of our new addition, I suggested that he buy himself a new vehicle too. I argued that the Bronco was on its last leg; he had never owned a brand-new vehicle, and most importantly, he deserved one. He contemplated the idea for a while. And one weekend, when I thought I was going to go out of my mind with worry because he was late in coming home from work, he pulled into the driveway with a brand-new champagne-colored extended-cab Chevy Truck. It was just as extraordinarily large and powerful as he was. I'm sure the neighbors thought we had won the lotto.

In unison, the children and I begged him for a ride. He was excited as a kid with a brand-new toy and happily obliged. His excitement was infectious. The kids cheered noisily as they climbed aboard. We practically needed a ladder to get inside. The interior was tan in color and smelled like new leather. We were so in awe of its newness and enormity that we hardly noticed the sting on our sweaty legs when they stuck to the seats. The dashboard looked like the control panel of an airplane. With a flip of a switch, Mark cooled our sweaty faces with a refreshing breeze of cold air. And then he turned on the surround-sound stereo. It was what we imagined being inside a limo was like. Going on errands would never be the same again. My final goal was to obtain a professional job. By the end of the summer, with the help from career counselors at the college and Mark's editing expertise, I created a resume. Because I hadn't worked since my children were born, over ten years prior, it didn't look all that impressive as it mostly consisted of education. The best job I could get without much work experience—not at all related to what I was trained to do—was as an administrative assistant at Virginia Mason Medical Center in downtown Seattle. Mark was proud of me nonetheless and called me at least twice a day to remind me that he was and went so far as to have fresh cut flowers delivered to my office every two weeks. I was proud of myself too. Now among the ranks of the work force, I was officially released from governmental dependency. Ironically, I was no better off financially than I was before, but I was manning the helm alone, and that was what mattered most.

No More Nights in the Alley

*E*very day, I left my new car at the Northgate Park and Ride and commuted to work by Metro. I rode Mark's bus route as our work shifts would allow. Sometimes his bus would find me as I headed home at the end of the day. Once in awhile, he took his breaks at the park and ride, where my car was parked, and would leave gifts and/or cards for me on my driver's seat. Although they were sporadic surprises, they always came when I needed cheering up the most. Of all the different types of cards he left, there was one in particular that caught me off guard. It wasn't so unusual that it had a picture of a cat on it since he and I both loved cats, but this cat happened to be dressed in a wedding gown. The caption read *No More Nights in the Ally*. It didn't take long before I figured out what the meaning of the message was. When I spoke with him later, he confirmed my assumptions. He said it was time. And before I could begin to comprehend what he was getting at, he asked if the following weekend would be a good time to make arrangements for a moving truck. Dumfounded, speechless, excited, and nervous all at the same time, my mind raced around and around. Was I ready? What could I say? This was what we had been working toward all along, and I gave him my promise after all.

Throwing caution to the wind, we rented a moving truck the following weekend. Because I lived in a third-story walk-up, it took the efforts of all six of us to move everything through the narrow hallways and twist and turns of my apartment. Because we owned double of what Mark had at his house, we didn't need to take as many things. I either threw the extra stuff away or we took it to the Goodwill. And what was still in good condition was saved for a yard sale. What we brought to his house was mainly personal possessions all within a few boxes. As we settled in for our first night *home*, I couldn't help but think that this was the riskiest thing I had ever done. I gave up nearly everything I had worked so hard for, including my independence, all for the love of this man.

Living under the same roof with a blended family, in a teeny-tiny house, was eventful to say the least. The three bedrooms were especially small. There was discord among the ranks when we decided to move his eldest, from his room, to the den and give Lex his room and move Dale into his youngest's room. But Mark always knew how to make it fun. To keep the peace, we spent as little time in the house as possible and continued with the traditions and routines we created together—weekend outings and family time. Mark made another major change. He insisted that he and the children would do most of the chores. He said now that I lived in his house, I had to let him take care of me—"nonnegotiable, zip, end of it." He further explained that I should involve myself in the more enjoyable things I loved to do like reading or sewing. His proposal was foreign to me and definitely not something I would ever get used to, and I only gave in to it when he was at home.

Just when I thought I knew Mark well enough, I learned even more while living with him. Not only did he feed the wild animals away from home, but he also fed any animal that ventured into his back porch. Of the masses that stopped by Mark's twenty-four-hour diner were wild squirrels and blue jays that, along with their friends and families, were dependant and expectant of their daily feedings. The squirrels trusted him so much that they would take the nuts from his hand and eat them at his feet. He spent as much money on animal food, wild and domestic, as he did on food for his family. He bought at least ten pounds of peanuts every week—not the cheaper ones in the bulk bin mind you but the specialty kind in bags that cost four dollars each. Every other day, he bought five pounds of wild birdseed to take to work with him. And every other week, he bought fancy, dehydrated corncob sticks that he would pound into the deck railing for all of the animals. It wasn't long before they invited themselves into the house cats or no cats. We even caught one sitting in the coffee can where the peanuts were kept! After that incident, the back door remained closed at all times; or else who knew what other kind of wild animals would make themselves at home.

Not always Saint Francis of Assisi with the wild animals, Mark detested the opossums and the raccoons. Whenever he saw one of those critters on his back porch, his personality would switch like Dr. Jekyll and Mr. Hyde. In a maniacal split second, he'd grab an M1000 from a drawer next to the back door, light it, and throw it out after them just as they were hightailing it down the back cliff. When it exploded, the whole backyard would light up, and the aftershocks could be felt from within the house—and, I'm certain, throughout the neighborhood. The kids, feeding on his frenzy, would go crazy with excitement, laughing and screaming the entire time. Oddly enough, the neighbors never complained. Of the domestic animals, he absolutely loved cats, and he most definitely disliked dogs except for the husky he once had. We eventually ended up with four cats. Two he had for several years, Omar and Cinder-Mamma kitty; and two that were adopted from my sister, Dinky and Amos.

In the fall, we enrolled my children in the local elementary school and began making more plans for our future. First and foremost, we planned to have our wedding the following spring, May 15, 1999. With his mom's blessing, the ceremony was to be held at her house; and of course, the Armadillo restaurant would be the caterers. With a wedding-planning book, I made notes for ideas and collected things for the big day. Because decorating was his sister's specialty, she helped me with ideas for setting *the stage*. I hoped to include a unity candle in the ceremony; but after several stores, I couldn't find the perfect one. Nearly defeated, I made a final stop at a local Christian store to see what was there. Tucked back in the corner, I found a display of candles. As I approached them, the hairs on my neck stood up and sent chills down the center of my back. I stopped and stared. I couldn't believe what I saw. It wasn't the beauty of the pure white unity candle adorned with faux pearls and lace that stood out but what was written on the packaging that caught my attention. In bold letters across the top was the manufactures name—Lillian Rose. It was the very name that we chose for a baby if we were to have a girl someday. Lillian, after his favorite aunt, and Rose after his mom. I was convinced that it was a sign. In addition to a fitting scripture—1 Corinthians 13:4-8—on the front, it sold itself. I rushed home to show it to Mark.

Once settled in our new home, the gestures of love Mark showed me were even greater than they ever were before. When I arrived home from work each night, he would have me sit on my favorite chair, prop my feet up on a footstool with a pillow, and enjoy something cold to drink. I was always glad to accept. Occasionally, he would light candles and have a warm-scented bath waiting for me. And when I finished, I would find my pajamas folded and waiting for me on my side of the bed still warm from the dryer. And as if that wasn't enough, Mark would lie on my side for a little while so I always had a warm bed to climb into. I told him that he made me feel special like royalty. As always, he'd laugh and say, "Yeah, a royal highnass." As much as I tried to relax like he wanted me to and to enjoy my new life, I couldn't; all this seemed just too good to be true.

With November, just after my thirty-third birthday, came the news of a departmental layoff at my new job to occur at the end of the year. And my name was on the list. "Last one in, first one out," they said. Ever confident and always seeing life as a glass half full, Mark assured me that it wasn't crucial that I find another job right away. But because he understood my intrinsic need for independence, he helped me to prepare for job hunting once again. Meanwhile, I took a weekend job as a cashier at J. C. Penny's. Because the job was flexible, I was able to choose which weekends I wanted to work. And because Mark had some paid time off to use, we decided to celebrate my birthday the second weekend of the month. We settled on a trip to Canada and to share some of our celebration with his Canadian relatives. As was his way, we rented what he referred to as a *big butt* car, a brand-new white Cadillac, and drove comfortably and in style all the way to Vancouver. Although his family insisted that we stay with them, Mark opted to take me to the Weston Hotel instead. I'll never forget walking through the enormous elegant hallways of the hotel and wondering what might be going through the minds of those who saw us. We both were wearing sweats and tennis shoes, and in addition to our luggage, Mark carried several transparent plastic grocery bags full of saltine crackers boxes. We must have looked like some poor folks who just won a night's stay at the hotel and couldn't afford anything else to eat.

After a night on the town, Mark and I decided to go for a swim in the hotel's swimming pool. Feeling self-conscious in a swimsuit, I told him I wouldn't get in if there were other people swimming. He assured me that we would be alone since it was late in the evening. But that was not the case when we got there. Several people were still in the pool. Without reservation, Mark took off his robe and sauntered innocently to the side of the pool, acting as if he were about to jump in. The pool instantly vacated. I couldn't believe it. I burst into a fit of laughter. As he said, we would have the entire pool to ourselves. I felt like a little kid when I jumped into the water with him. I wrapped my arms around his neck and gave him a big wet kiss on his cheek. Like a maternal gorilla, he swung me around to his back and pulled me all around the pool. Time seemed to stand still as we laughed, splashed, and played. We had a great time—no pressures and no responsibilities. Later that night, we watched a movie, the remake of *Dr. Doolittle* with Eddie Murphy, and barely made it to the end before dropping off into a deep, sound sleep.

Early the next morning, I was rudely awakened by the sound of hundreds of screeching gulls—not unlike the sound from an Alfred Hitchcock movie. When I looked toward the source of the noise, I saw Mark standing on the balcony, flinging saltine crackers at the gulls like a skeet shooter. With an evil laugh, he asked if I wanted to join him. As I approached the balcony, I saw many of our neighbors standing out on their balconies and glaring at him. Embarrassed, I decided to forgo participating in his maniacal ritual. Later that day, we joined his favorite aunt, Lil, and her family for dim sum, walked through Stanley Park with his cousin, and then headed back home. We had so much fun; it was a memorable birthday for sure.

We were home for just a short while when we learned that his mom had only months to live. Mark had the children wait in the living room as he quietly led me to our bedroom. He lay down on the bed, took me in his arms, and softly cried. My heart ached for him. I'd never seen him cry before, or any man cry for that matter. I didn't know what to do. Helpless, I held him as close as I could and cried with him and thought about the challenge that lay ahead. After a while, we shared the news with our children.

Chapter Two: A Love Story

The following week was a short workweek for both of us because of the upcoming holiday. Although it wasn't the week for my customary flower delivery, Mark made a surprise visit to my office with Safeway flowers, following his appointment with the dentist. He had to make his visit brief because he had to return to work. Safeway flowers and a personal visit by my Hunny Bunny—no matter how short—was definitely a fair trade for a flower delivery.

Thanksgiving was soon upon us. As always, it was split several different ways. Mark's children would visit with their mom for a while, and we would visit with my mom until it was time to pick them up. Then we would have dinner at his mom's with his family. The following day, Mark, the kids, and I would have our own holiday dinner at home. Although the plans and arrangements were the same, that year's celebration was different. Because of the knowledge that it might be the last Thanksgiving shared with his mom weighing in the back of everyone's minds, it was especially difficult for anyone to be in the holiday spirit. On the way to his mom's house, I hoped to distract the kids by asking them what each of them was most thankful for. But before anyone could respond, Mark did me one better by bellowing "Good gas!" followed by a tremendous evil laugh, which was then followed by screeching laughter and armpit farts from the kids. I most definitely lost that one. I never did find out what everyone was most thankful for.

More relatives visited that year than before. Choosing to ignore the reality and seriousness of her fate, his mom went about dinner like she did every year—smiling, laughing, and joking—with not a care in the world. The kids played with the other relatives while the adults visited. Everything was as it usually was. And what we thought was going to be a solemn Thanksgiving turned out to be one of the better ones. Because Mark and I worked the following day, it was decided that Lexi would stay the night with his mom and his sister. So with a final round of hugs and kisses for all, Mark, the boys, and I headed for home. As we drove, I couldn't help but think how devastated and depressed Mark was going to be without his mom, and how learning to live without her was to be our greatest challenge yet.

*   *   *

Chapter Three: The Morning After

The Morning After

There's got to be a morning after
If we can hold on through the night
We have a chance to find the sunshine
Let's keep on looking for the light
Oh, can't you see the morning after?
It's waiting right outside the storm
Why don't we cross the bridge together
And find a place that's safe and warm?
It's not too late; we should be giving
Only with love can we climb
It's not too late, not while we're living
Let's put our hands out in time
There's got to be a morning after
We're moving closer to the shore
I know we'll be there tomorrow
And we'll escape the darkness
We won't be searching anymore
There's got to be a morning after . . .

Numb

$\mathcal{D}$aylight filled the room. I stretched sleepily across the bed in search of Mark to pull him closer to me. Not finding him, I figured that he was up already. My eyes hurt when I tried to open them. Understanding why, terror grasped my heart like an unforgiving vice as the events of the day before spun around my mind like scenes from a scary movie. Seeking comfort from his side of the bed, I gathered his pillow to my chest and cried myself back to sleep. I awoke again sometime later to the sound of someone inside my house. I still can't recall who was there, but they called to me in a sweet and soothing voice. I couldn't shake the dreamlike trance I was in. Everything seemed to be happening in slow motion. Consolingly and patiently, she directed me through the motions of dressing and preparing for the day. I felt brain-dead.

She drove me to the house of Mark's mom where Lexi was waiting for me. My appearance seemed to frighten her. She approached me hesitantly and then hugged me gently. I sat at the kitchen table. His children were there as well. They didn't approach me. There was lots of activity in the house with people dropping by to offer their condolences and to leave warm food dishes for the family. Every now and again, I heard someone say, to those requesting to see me, "She's not up for visiting right now." News reports of the tragedy blared repeatedly on the television. Hours later, I was brought back to my house. My sister took Lexi and Dale home with her. For several days, the same person came to my house. Each day, she'd walk me through the same routine and then drive me, in silence, to the house of Mark's mom. I didn't understand why I had to go every day, but I went. Each time, I took my place at the kitchen table near the window where I could see Whidbey Island in the far distance, evidence that the fairy tale had once existed. Occasionally, unexpected tears would well up in my eyes and stream down my face. Wanting to detach myself from the world that continued to move around me, I stared mindlessly and blindly into space until I was taken home again. What I wanted was just to be left alone. What I wanted was to stay in bed until I withered away and died. What I wanted most was Mark.

I found peace within the safety of our home, but the reminders were there too. Every day that I was returned home, I was greeted by several business cards, wedged into the cracks of our front door, from various news media with requests to interview me; but the possibility of that ever happening was inconceivable. Because our phone number was listed in the local directory, our phone rang constantly, flooding our answering machine with messages. Eventually, I yanked both of them from the wall just to make it all stop, to keep the outside from coming in. Occasionally, flowers and letters of condolence were left on the porch too. Letters came to me from every which way. To read them seemed only to remind me of what I was so determined to deny. I didn't open a single one. I tucked them all lovingly and safely away for *someday* instead. The food, the flowers, the notes from strangers—so many affected, like ripples in the water, by that the same senseless act on that horrible day—and as much as I wanted to separate myself from it all, I was uplifted by their thoughtfulness at the same time.

Eventually, the day came when funeral clothes for Mark had to be assembled. I sat at the end of our bed and stared—for what seemed to be an eternity—at our closet. I just couldn't comprehend what I was supposed to do. I never put his clothes out for him before. Mark always dressed himself. He either wore his work uniform, sweats or shorts, and T-shirts. I never had seen him in a suit before or *monkey suit* as he would have referred to it. We hadn't even bought his tux for the wedding yet. Anything formal would have to be custom-made. Struggling with my thoughts, I said aloud, "A funeral, what would you wear to a funeral?" I was jolted back to reality when his side of the closet door began to shake violently. In a trance, indifferent to what had just occurred, I responded and slid open the door. I searched methodically and eventually found a dress shirt and a blazer that might fit him. He wore the same set a few years earlier for his eldest sister's funeral, but I couldn't find any pants. I explained my dilemma to his family. The funeral home director told them that this could be resolved by keeping the lower half of Mark covered during services thereby omitting the need for pants.

Procedure

The day after the tragedy, a man from the Big Brother's program, Jim, brought Dale to the scene of *ground zero*. Dale wanted to put flowers on Daddy Mark's chair. Metro officials welcomed him and were more than happy to postpone towing the wreckage for a few more minutes. They lifted the crime-scene tape for Dale. With Jim close behind, they boarded the mangled bus. In silence, they stood and stared at the empty driver's seat. Choking back tears, Dale bravely placed his bouquet of flowers on the seat. They stepped off the bus together and watched while the bus was towed away.

Eventually, Mark's belongings were returned to his mom. Any money he had in his possession was given to his boys. I asked for and was given the key chain I gave him for his birthday years before and his workbag. The bag was black and made of a parachute type of material and Velcro. It didn't suffer any damage, just the usual wear and tear. I carefully unzipped each of its pockets to investigate the insides. Among the things I found, all neatly organized, were a wad of napkins, a bundle of rubber bands, his *route bible*, bus transfers, schedules, a run card, and other work-related stuff. I laughed when I came across some holistic medicine that he had been using. He referred to my naturopathic medicine as all hocus-pocus. After carefully inspecting every little nook and cranny, I zipped all the pockets closed again, careful to leave everything as he left it. Sadly though, the little doll Lex gave him was gone. I wiped the tears that trickled down my cheeks; I mourned for the doll too.

Although his workbag might seem trivial to others, it was priceless to me, and I would treasure it always. His workbag seemed to work a little magic on his eldest sister's cat—a chubby cream-colored, orange-and-white tabby named Marmalade—that his mother inherited. She wouldn't let anyone near her except for Mark; she just loved him. Whenever he visited, she would plop herself at his feet and shamelessly roll all over the floor until he stopped whatever he was doing and pet her. On the day his workbag arrived at his mom's, she somehow knew it was his. She watched me intently while I inspected its contents. And immediately, upon setting it down, she proceeded to roll all over it and purr her loudest. I was even more startled by what she did next. Without hesitation, she ran directly to me and jumped on my lap, rolling around haphazardly and nearly falling off. Occasionally, she'd stop to nudge my hands to pet her. Eventually, her loud purring evolved into a low consoling purr as she downshifted to settle in. And there she stayed until I left and every day I visited thereafter. It seemed as if it was her way of saying that she missed him too.

Almost immediately, efforts to clean up the tragedy scene and repair damages were well under way. The media continued repeatedly to air the details. Someone taped a single teardrop under one of the troll's eyes. A shrine of flowers and candles covered its lap. And a photo, cut from the newspaper, of Mark and I had been enlarged and taped onto one of the bridge's supports. A shrine of flowers and candles were placed respectably below it. For a few days following the tragedy, King County facilities flew their flags at half-staff in respectful memory of Mark. There was a table set up at all the transit bases for mourners to leave cards and donations or to write remembrances for his family in a journal. Metro also designed a Web page for mourners' thoughts and condolences.

Arrangements and Planning

*T*he cacophonic atmosphere of visitors and media subsided just a little, just enough, for funeral arrangements to be made. Mark's family organized the details and, occasionally, ran them by me to see what I thought; but I chose not to be part of it. I believed that if I didn't go along with the idea that he died, somehow and in someway, it would make it untrue. All that crazy thinking stopped the day Barry Samet, the president of the union that represented all the Metro employees, became a part of my life. Although he was a kind and funny man, he was also firm in everything he believed in. True to his word, he took it upon himself to assure that I was involved in the planning of Mark's memorial service whether I wanted to or not.

Barry was determined not to let me sit idly by and wither away. Unlike others who might ask me a question and then politely walk away if I didn't feel like answering, he would stubbornly wait until I answered him. He wouldn't let me hide behind the curtain I put up for myself. And so, you can imagine how shocked I was the day he called to ask me how Mark would want to be remembered. I wanted the world to swallow me up. I argued angrily to myself, *Remembered? No, we're not going to* remember *him. Remembering him would mean that he's gone somewhere. No, we're not going to remember him!* A large lump formed in my throat. It ached worse than the tonsillectomy I had as a kid. I struggled to swallow past it to answer him. Unaffected by my display of defiance, Barry continued to wait patiently for my reply. Tears streamed down my face; the only answer I could mutter was, "Big."

The Viewing

*J*ust when I thought things couldn't get any worse came the day of the viewing. All day and into the evening, Mark's closest friends and family gathered at his mom's house and drove in little groups to the funeral home. Always invited to go along, I avoided the dreaded ritual by making the excuse that I wasn't ready yet. And just when I thought I had successfully missed out on it, my best friend arrived and, along with loving intervention from Mark's sister, I was coaxed into going even if it was the middle of the night. They stood on either side of me, with their arms wrapped securely and supportively around my waist, as we entered the building. The funeral home was inviting; it wasn't cold and indifferent as I had imagined it would be. It was too quiet, and the lights were dimmed. There were several lit candles placed strategically throughout the room, illuminating a tranquil ambiance that calmed my nerves some. My eyes searched anxiously around the room in apprehension of seeing Mark's body. But thankfully, he wasn't anywhere that I could see him.

The girls guided me toward a pair of large white double doors. Somehow, I knew that beyond them, I would find Mark. They each opened a side panel. Inside was yet another room— much darker, more solemn, and more foreboding than the foyer. They proceeded to guide me in. But my knees buckled, and my heart skipped a beat. The room became suddenly dry and thick, sucking the oxygen from my lungs. I gasped for air as I struggled to catch my breath. And to save myself from anymore unforeseen trauma, I dug my heels firmly into the carpet and cried, "No no no! Not yet! Not yet!" With love and patience and with their arms still securely around me, they gently and slowly guided me away from the room to a bench, just outside the door, where we all sat down together. They wiped the tears from my face, stroked my hair, and whispered consolingly to me.

When I thought I was ready to try again, holding fast to each of them, we stood together and walked toward the darker room once more. But again, I only made it as far as the threshold before fear—greater than anything I had ever feared before—shot through my body with lightning-bolt sharpness and caused my knees to buckle again. I just couldn't make myself go into that room even though my heart knew that I must. Again the girls patiently and supportively walked me back to the bench and sat with me until I felt ready to try once more. I don't know how many times we did this, but I eventually felt brave enough to make it past the threshold, allowing them to guide me to where

Chapter Three: The Morning After

Mark's body lay. There was a bench adjacent to his casket, and I sat next to him. Every bone in my body shook. I felt freezing cold. With wobbly knees, I took a deep breath and stood beside him. I reached out and touched his hands. He was so cold. I laid my head on his chest. It too was cold and hard as cement. *This wasn't my warm and snuggly Hunny Bunny lying here*, I thought to myself.

I leaned into the casket. I wrapped my arms around him and cried like I've never cried before. My tears made his face wet as I kissed his cheeks, his forehead, his nose, and his eyes. I nuzzled into the familiar nape of his neck and buried my face into his hair—seeking his warmth, his smell, and anticipating the stroke of his hands on my hair assuring me that everything was going to be all right. But nothing happened. I hugged him even tighter and cried even more. "No no no! Hunny Bunny, Hunny Bunny, please! Wake up! Wake up! Wake up!" I pleaded to him over and over again. I cried and I cried. The mournful sound of my wounded soul echoed eerily throughout the corridors of the funeral home. I cried until my throat, my jaw, my eyes, and my heart hurt. The girls were beside me again. I reached into my coat pocket. I brought out the Father's Day button the kids made for him years before and the guardian-angel key chain he always carried. With an unsteady hand, I secured the button onto his lapel and placed the key chain in his breast pocket. I kissed his face one more time and let the girls guide me out to the car and back to his mom's house.

That night, I fell into bed exhausted; but even as tired as I was, sleep eluded me. I had never felt so sick or so drained in my life. Every inch of my body ached, but none as much as my heart did. I occupied myself by trying to permanently etch in my mind every little detail of our nightly ritual. I never wanted to forget. I spoke aloud to the darkness, in hopes that Mark could hear me, "I miss the way you warmed my side of the bed. I miss hearing the sucking noises you made while you flossed your teeth. And the sounds you made while you brushed your teeth as you walked around the house, securing it for the night. And the loud noises you'd make spitting the depleted toothpaste into the sink and the even louder spitting and gargling noises as you swished the water inside your cheeks. And I miss the encore of one last and final sucking noise you made with your teeth on your way to bed."

I couldn't chase the image of Mark, lying in that coffin, out of my mind. I tried to rationalize everything that had happened so far. Nothing made sense. What once was a bright and promising future now was covered by a secretive cloak of darkness. My heart ached when I thought of the years we worked so hard to bring our lives together. I cursed myself for the precious time I wasted with my stubborn independence. I mourned too for our daughter, Lillian Rose, who would never be. I sought his pillow for comfort but discovered that his scent had worn away and found only sorrow instead. Unafraid of the stillness of the night or the footsteps I heard pacing just outside our bedroom door, I found comfort instead and drifted into a deep sleep.

The Family's Memorial

*T*he days and nights since the tragedy blended together in a sea of tears. I felt as if I had drifted farther and farther away from Mark. And the farther I drifted, the more exposed and insecure I felt. Soon the night of the family's memorial service was before me. I allowed Dale to be a part of the services but not Lexi. I felt that she was still too young to understand. It was also the day that the King County Credit Union erected their Christmas tree in Mark's honor and the beginning of their fundraiser of handmade Christmas ornaments for his memorial fund. And it was the day that King County executive Ron Sims officially retired the bus route number 359 in Mark's honor and had route 358 take its place.

The media was swarming again when we arrived at the church. They asked how we were, but how do you answer such a question? Mark and I were private people—unknowns until now. I felt as if I was in a fishbowl and all eyes were on me, watching and judging my reactions. In all honesty, I didn't know exactly what my reactions were supposed to be. I didn't know how to do this. At times, I felt like crying. As much as I fought back the tears for fear that it was *too much*, it was no use. I had no control of my emotions; they just came at will. Unsure if it was appropriate to smile at well-wishers, I stared at them blankly. And even worse were the moments when I should have been crying that my tears were dried up. What came out instead were more like moans of a wounded animal. Adding insult to injury, causing me even more anxiety, was when I overheard someone say, "She really puts on a great show, huh?"

Several hundred mourners came to pay their respects and to offer their condolences. Because there wasn't enough room in the church, they had to televise the service in another building. Although I knew they meant well, I resented the words "I'm sorry for your loss" and "It's better to have loved and lost, dear, than to have never loved at all." Those words echoed menacingly in my head like the chants from the children who taunted me in elementary school. It took every ounce of self-discipline I had not to scream and lash out at every person who uttered them as if all of this was their fault. Among the mourners were dozens of Mark's Metro colleagues. Each wore black armbands and black buttons with Mark's work ID number, 2106, printed in white on them. As well, many longtime passengers and some of his friends from his high school days came to pay their respects. I felt really proud for Mark. I'm sure he had no idea just how many lives he touched.

At seven PM, coinciding with the start of the services, Rick Walsh, Metro's general manager, requested—over every Metro coach's PA system—all of the operators to stop their buses at the safest location and pause for a brief tribute to Mark following with a one-minute moment of silence. The memorial service was as surreal as it was overwhelming. The church was decorated beautifully. In an honorable display by the priest's podium, propped up for everyone to see, was his photograph, flowers, wreaths, and personal mementos. Among them was the picture I had sewn for his fortieth birthday. As I turned over his funeral announcement, I was pleasantly surprised with what I found. There at the bottom, in a cameo photograph, was an exact replica of his little lost doll—his precious Dollface. Even more tears welled up in my eyes. The endearment meant more to me than the person who placed it there would ever know.

His sister and I clung to each other throughout the services. I managed to stand proud for Mark even though my knees threatened to buckle. I maintained composure throughout most of the service but found it most difficult to keep the tears at bay whenever someone spoke of things that they would most remember Mark for. After the priest blessed Mark and everyone in the room, he led the procession out of the church. Each family member placed a single rose on Mark's coffin as it passed by and then quietly filed out behind it in procession for the viewing followed by the rest of the mourners. A reception was held in the church reception hall. I couldn't take being around so many people one more minute nor did I want to be approached by the media. So my best friend snuck me out the back door of the church and into her car. Against her better judgment, she reluctantly dropped me off at my house. It seemed as if wanting to be alone wasn't an appropriate reaction either. I couldn't understand what was wrong with wanting to be left alone. It seemed as though all anybody wanted to talk about was the day of the tragedy or how I was feeling. I didn't want to remember it. I didn't want to talk about it. I didn't want to talk about anything at all.

Home alone at last, I stood in our dimly lit living room and spoke once again to the empty space, "I remember, when you came home from work, you'd go directly to our room and quickly strip out of your uncomfortable work clothes as if you were shedding the shackles of the day. And once free from their confinement, you'd comically dance around naked while gleefully announcing that you were doing the 'dangle.'" And then I laughed, the first time in what seemed an eternity, and continued my conversation with Mark. "Then, after your brief moment of insanity, you'd put on your cotton shorts and a tank top and head for the kitchen. You never wanted what the kids and I had for dinner, and sometimes that hurt my feelings. You said your stomach couldn't handle a heavy meal late at night, and that you'd rather have popcorn instead. I remember how you armed yourself with your popcorn, a big glass of ice water, your favorite tattered pale green pillow, and your newspaper and find a comfortable spot on the living room floor to unwind. And how, even if sometimes the children and I interrupted your downtime with incessant chatter or the cats would lay in the middle of your paper—though you rarely got any time to yourself except when you were doing the *Archie Bunker*—you never complained. And I remember how you especially loved the times that I rubbed your feet while you relaxed. I never did soften that hard patch just underneath your large toe." With a heavy heart, I reluctantly returned to the present and walked to the hall closet in search of another scented shirt of Mark's. I found his flannel shirt coat, the one that he wore when he worked out in the yard, the same one he wore every year to chop down our Christmas tree. It was the last of his clothing with his scent on it. I wrapped the coat around his pillow, curled myself around it, and drifted in and out of sleep.

The Burial

I dreamt that Mark and I were sitting on a park bench and talking. It didn't seem like a dream. It felt real. I could see and hear him as clear as day. He laughed at my continual string of questions but patiently answered each and every one of my concerns. Before I could tell him goodbye, I woke up. I struggled to fall back to sleep. I wanted to continue with our visit. My mind kept me awake, racing and searching frantically in every corner of my brain and trying my best to hold on to everything he had said. But all was lost. For the life of me, I just couldn't remember what he said.

Like our favorite movie, *Groundhog Day*, the same morning seemed to come over and over again, cruelly reminding me of what I fought so hard to deny. It seemed as if I couldn't think of anything else, as if I had forgotten all of my life before *it* happened. This particular morning brought Mark's burial.

Mark McLaughlin
Memorial

December 8, 1998
Key Arena - Seattle

Greater Seattle Pipe Band
Presentation of Colors - King County Sheriff's Honor Guard
National Anthem
Opening Prayer - Dr. Thomas Pousche, Chaplain ATU Local 775
Welcome - Barry Samet, ATU 587 President
Glen Travis, ATU 587 Vice President
Musical Selection by Men Without Kilts & Lasses Fair
Speakers - U.S. Senator, Patty Murray
King County Executive, Ron Sims
Metro Base Chief, Abdul Alidina
Operator & Friend, Stan Green
Mike McLaughlin
Eulogy - Dr. Pousche
Musical Selection by Gunnear Goerlitz
Presentation of Flags to the McLaughlin Family
Amazing Grace - Greater Seattle Pipe Band
Taps - Deputy David Jeffries

There is no armor against fate
Death lays his icy hand on kings

Mark Francis McLAUGHLIN

Born June 13, 1954, in Seattle; died November 27, 1998 in Seattle. Mark was a Seattle native who loved the Pacific Northwest. He attended Christ the King grade school, Ingraham High School, served in the United States Army, and worked for Metro Transit for the past 19 years, dying in a tragic accident while on duty. Mark was a kind, generous man who always put others before himself. His death was a needless tragedy that has challenged his family and friends to continue his spirit of good humor and his love of life. He loved the outdoors and was happiest hiking in the mountains along the Robe Valley, or walking on the beach. He was kind to animals, a lover of music, and was always there to lend a hand to anyone in need. Above all, he was an incredibly devoted father who cherished his children and his fiancee's children. He was preceded in death by his father, Francis John McLaughlin and his sister, Dana Weller. Survived by his sons, Brad and Joel; his fiancee and best friend, Elise (Lis) Crawford, and her children, Dale and Lexi; by his mother, Rose McLaughlin; his brothers, Michael McLaughlin and Terry Weller; and his sister, Debra McLaughlin. In lieu of flowers, donations may be made to a memorial fund for Brad and Joel c/o The Mark McLaughlin Fund at any Washington Mutual Bank Branch; or donations may be made in Mark's name to P.A.W.S., PO Box 1037, Lynnwood, WA. 98046. We love you Mark. Funeral Mass will be celebrated Thursday, December 3, 1998, at 7 p.m. at **Christ the King Catholic Church.** Viewing will be from 6 p.m. to 6:45 p.m. and for 30 minutes after Mass. A burial procession will form and leave from Christ the King Church, North 117th Street and Dayton Ave. North, Friday, December 4th, at 10 a.m., for the burial at **Holyrood Cemetery**, 205 Northeast 205th St., Shoreline.

HOFFNER FISHER & HARVEY

Obituary

Mark's memorial bus

The family bus

In solidarity

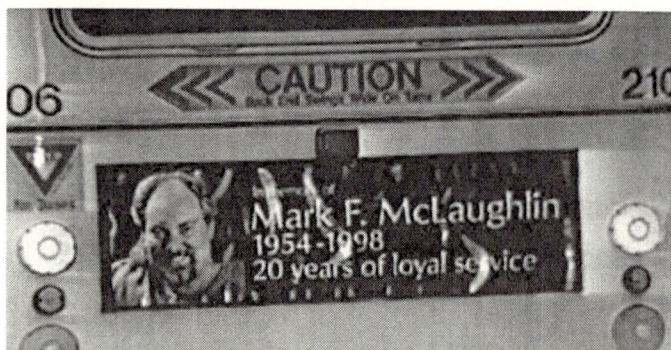

Mark F. McLaughlin
1954-1998
20 years of loyal service

Salute to a hero

Mark's buddies   Thousands come

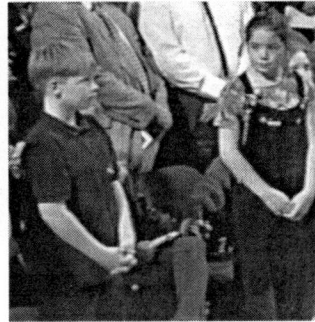

US Senator Patty Murray,
King County executive Ron Sims,
and King County councilmember Louise Miller

Rick Walsh, Metro Transit's general manager

Eulogy - Dr. Thomas Pousche,
Chaplain ATU Local 775

Barry presents Mark's memorial flag to me

Gunnear plays Jimmy for Mark

I couldn't take it anymore. No sooner had I made it to the surface for air that another tidal wave would wash over to suffocate me again. I wanted to stay in bed with the covers over my head. Every inch of my body ached; I felt like something the cat had dragged in and spit out. No, worse than that—what they had buried in their litter box. But hiding wasn't an option as I heard my guardian angel arrive, once again, to pull me back into the world of the living. Reluctantly, I prepared myself physically for the long day ahead. Funeral clothes were not in my wardrobe either so I settled for a black pair of slacks and a blouse. The temperature was just above freezing. The wind was calm. It was an overcast, gloomy morning as the family assembled at house of Mark's mom. Again Dale was with me, and Lex stayed with my sister. It was decided that the boys, including Dale and Mark's brothers, would be the pallbearers. Several black limousines arrived. This was not how I planned my first ride in one. The drivers escorted us to the sedans. The sedan distracted the children momentarily as they excitedly explored the inside of it. I wanted them to sit still, to be respectful, but I reminded myself that they were just children after all. When I saw the multitudes of people gathering at the church, I was thankful that the sedan had dark windows.

Eventually, the car stopped, and the doors were opened. To my horror, a hand reached inside and motioned for me to come out. I did not want to go. It was the wife of Mark's younger brother. With sympathy and understanding, she coaxed me out of the car and explained that we were to see Mark one last time. We rushed past the crowd into the church. The family gathered around the casket. I stood next to his eldest brother who flew in from California for the services. The priest said some final blessings and began to close the casket. I lost it. I felt my legs collapse. I grabbed on to the eldest brother's arm with one hand and reached for Mark with the other. His brother put his arms around me and whispered consolingly, "You have to let him go now." Again, like the wounded animal that had taken permanent residency in my soul, I could hear myself crying. It seemed not to come from my throat but from somewhere deep within my heart. I couldn't control it. "No no no! Hunny Bunny, noooo!" Lovingly but firmly, his brother pulled me back so the casket could be closed. Mark's sister-in-law assisted me back to the car.

I was already a mess, and we hadn't even had the burial yet. The children stared at me. I turned away from them and looked out the window. I chastised myself for the way I was reacting or overreacting. I felt for Dale. He had never seen me behave like this before. I tried to give myself some credit. I mean, how was I to prepare? Would I have reacted differently had I known ahead of time? I rationalized that the moments I became hysterical was over something that I wasn't prepared for. Crazy thoughts like these raced around and around in my head. I might as well have had some boxing gloves to hit myself with. In an attempt to brighten my mood some, Dale pointed toward the back window and told me to look. I couldn't believe what I saw. Following behind us, as far as the eye could see, was a convoy of Metro buses and vans, official vehicles, and other mourners in vehicles of various shapes and sizes. Driving along either side and in the front of us were several police officers on motorcycles. At every intersection all along the six-mile procession to the cemetery, police officers stopped traffic to allow the massive convoy to pass. It was impressive. The heaviness in my heart lightened a little, and I smiled encouragingly at Dale.

Once at the cemetery, I was joined by his mom. Arm in arm, we walked in quiet reverence to our seats next to the burial site. My heart ached for her. She walked this same path not long ago, burying both a husband and a daughter in the same place where her favorite son was about to be put to rest and where she herself would soon rest alongside them. We waited quietly as the pallbearers brought Mark's coffin to rest in front of us. Although Dale was the smallest, he walked proud and brave as he effortlessly helped to carry the coffin of the only *father* he had ever known. I was certain that this would be the most difficult thing he would ever have to do. I was so proud of him. My best friend stood behind me and placed her hands supportively on my shoulders, and I somehow managed to maintain composure throughout the entire ceremony. Afterward, all the family and friends gathered at his mom's, many of whom I had never met. I sensed a cold indifference from his family; something had changed. Even here, my home away from home, I felt awkward and uncomfortable. I had my best friend take me home. I missed the kids. I needed their distraction. I called my sister and asked if she would bring them home. She was more than happy to oblige. It seemed as if the presence of the children was all the indicator the neighbors needed to know that it was all right to visit. I didn't realize how many wonderful neighbors we had, but I certainly had the distraction I sought. For a while, there was always someone dropping by to bring us food and conversation. Occasionally, they left flowers and letters of condolences on my front steps. And one time, the children found stuffed animals waiting for them on our back porch. Never once did anyone talk about *it*, and little did they know that brought me more comfort than anything else.

Having the children home gave me purpose. I thought less of how miserable I was by caring for them. Although I managed through each and every day, there was one thing that I just couldn't do, and that was to keep the house warm. Mark had previously dismantled all of the wall heaters in the house and so the only source of heat was from a potbelly black woodstove. Everyone had a theory and or method—going to great lengths to show me, step by step, the fine art of fire making—how to make that thing work. But I couldn't get that miserable monster started for the life of me. Mark's friends brought wood and kindling and stacked it neatly in our driveway. But even with the best of intentions, I still couldn't make a fire. Kicking, yelling at it, and hitting it with an iron poker didn't make it work either. When did I become so helpless? Thankfully—before I caused too much damage—a neighbor and her husband dropped by every morning to light a fire for us. The house stayed warm for most of the day, but the nights were freezing. To keep warm, the children and I would cuddle in our bed in a heap of arms, legs, blankets, and pillows where they'd fall soundly asleep like newborn kittens and where I would lay awake, dreading the dawning of a new day—of the same reality. Images of Mark lying in that casket and lying beneath the cold, wet ground haunted my efforts to sleep. He did not like to be cold nor did he like to be dirty. These thoughts haunted my ability to sleep, and I spent the long hours of the night exhaustively tossing and turning.

The Public's Memorial

*I*t wasn't long before I faced yet another memorial for Mark. This one was for all Metro employees and the public. Barry was the mastermind behind it. When the day arrived, the family gathered, as usual, at the home of Mark's mom; this time, I allowed Lexi to come. Metro officials picked us up in company vans and brought us downtown to Metro's South Base. From there, they escorted us onto a waiting bus. To my great surprise, Barry and his wife joined us. The bus was older. The type I remember riding on when I was young. It was painted a pretty fire-engine red. Mark's badge number was displayed on the directional sign, and a funeral wreath was attached to the front of the bus.

I was amazed by what I saw next. As the driver brought our bus around the street side of the base, I saw the most beautifully decorated bus. It was exactly the same model as the last one Mark drove. The model number was the same as Mark's ID number, 2106. A black wreath adorned the front. Mark's picture, with his memorial and a message thanking him for twenty years of service, was displayed on either side of it. Mark's work jacket was draped on the back of the driver's seat with a black ribbon affixed to it. Purple ribbons were tied to the top of some of the passenger seats, representing the survivors of the tragedy. A sole black ribbon among them memorialized the one passenger who died. There wasn't a ribbon for the shooter. Black memorial flags—with Mark's badge number, 2106, printed in white on them—were posted on either side of the front of the bus. The driver's seat remained empty; it was pulled along instead by a tow truck bearing another memorial wreath. Along with two Seattle police officers on motorcycles for escorts, the procession began.

Following the memorial bus, we pulled out into the street. I saw behind us yet another bus, carrying Metro officials with a similar memorial wreath. And yet another bus followed behind that one, carrying Metro drivers and employees, and yet another followed that one carrying the same. Every single one of them carried memorial wreaths and bore Mark's ID number on their directional signs. Some even had notes of condolences written on their bulletin boards on either side of their buses. To my disbelief, the bus brigade stretched out beyond what I could see. I couldn't even begin to count them all. Barry said there must be eighty or more from all around the region—nationally and Canada. He said there were area fire engines and various transit vans following us too. I felt as excited as the kids. But I didn't dare show it. I wasn't sure what my reactions were supposed to be so I sat alone in my seat in quiet, stoic reverence.

We traveled slowly up Fourth Avenue. The bus brigade followed behind us in two columns side by side in silent solidarity. Crowds lined up on either side of the street. Some people carried signs, thanking the drivers. Some cried, and some saluted. Some placed their hands over their hearts. And nearly everyone waved. Even the Seattle firefighters stood by their fire engines in solemn salute. I'll always be eternally grateful for the love they showed for Mark and for all the Metro drivers. Lexi was beside herself; she wanted to know what was going on. I explained to her as best as I could in words that I hoped she could understand. Undaunted, squealing in delight, she ran to the window and waved to every person we passed as if to thank them all for their show of respect for her Daddy Mark. Her smiles and laughter were infectious, brightening the mood inside the bus. Dale soon joined in, saluting back those who saluted the bus.

The procession ended at the KeyArena. Mark's memorial service was to be held inside. His name and memorial announcement were written in lights on a sign adjacent to the building. When the bus stopped, I gave Barry a great big hug and thanked him. I told him that Mark would have loved all of this. Before we left the bus, Barry gave each of us a black memorial tack pin and button with Mark's number, 2106, printed in white on them. We were escorted into the arena toward a stage where a memorial was set up for Mark. My heart skipped a beat when my eyes caught sight of the larger-than-life photograph of Mark's *family*; it only included Mark and his boys. As we walked closer and closer to it, I felt a familiar sense of foreboding—the same feeling I recently had at his mom's house. We were led to front-row seats facing the stage. Some five thousand people joined us in the remaining seats behind ours. This was beyond the *big* that I expected.

For the next two hours, Mark's fellow Metro colleagues paid tribute to him. For many who spoke at the service, the memorial was a tribute not only to an end, but also to a beginning. A public acknowledgment of the grief, pain, and horror of the tragedy brought neighbors and friends closer together even for just a brief while. Emotions ran the gamut for all who attended. There were moments when the speeches and the music played made us laugh and others that moved us to tears. Knowing the family was in full view of the public, I managed to keep my emotions in check for most of the service. It was the moment after the King County Honor Guard presented the memorial American flag to the family and taps was played, followed by the playing of the bagpipes, that I began to unravel. Holding my breath to keep the tears at bay, I listened as Barry announced Mark as the honorary Operator of the Year; he would have been so proud. And just when I thought I had made it through the service without a breakdown came an unexpected announcement that echoed eerily throughout the massive space. Over the KeyArena broadcast system, a dispatcher called out for Mark. "Operator 2106 . . . [static followed by a moment of silence], Operator 2106 . . . [static followed by a moment of silence], Operator 2106 . . . is now out of service." With the final confirmation, the call abruptly disconnected, and everyone lost it. There wasn't a dry eye in the house.

Finally, in the safety of our home, I went directly to my room, closed the door, flopped down on the bed, and buried my face into my pillow. Now alone and away from scrutinizing eyes, I allowed myself to scream and cry. I tried to convince myself that this all wasn't real; it wasn't happening. I was sure that I had been in a terrible car accident and was in a coma, having a horrible nightmare of *what if.* Turning toward the ever-present dark shadow in the corner of my room, I cried out angrily, "I know you were always proud of my inner strength, independence, and resilience. It was what you loved most about me. You are the only one who ever really loved me, who believed in me and accepted me for who I am. I have never had a problem with acceptance ever. I've

119

accepted the trials and tribulations of single motherhood, life on public transportation, and the humility and sacrifices of poverty. But please forgive me, Mark, this one is too much! This one I cannot do! I can't go on! I'm so lost! I can't survive without you! I miss you so much it hurts!" Letting my head fall back onto the pillow, I rolled over and buried my face into its softness once again and cried until I eventually fell into a sound sleep.

Exiled

*S*ometime later, the children crept cautiously into the room and gently woke me. They asked what we would be eating for dinner. As the fog cleared my head, I realized that I was still in the nightmare. I felt bad for them. They had never seen me cry before—not like this, not every day. I wish I could give them their mommy back. So as not to cause them any further concern, I climbed out of the bed and followed them to the kitchen. Thankfully, there were plenty of leftovers in the fridge. I fed them and stared numbly into space as they ate. From the corner of my eye, I noticed that they were watching to see if I was going to eat too. For their sake, I pretended to. Although I was starving, my stomach felt nauseous and in knots. The thought of food just made it worse.

Time marched selfishly along. Eventually, I felt well enough to resume driving. For some reason, driving made me more nervous than *before*, especially when the children were in the car. Even so, I somehow felt better. I liked being in the enclosed space and listening to music again. Whenever a song Mark liked played on the radio, the children would yell, "Turn it up! Turn it up!—I wish I was in Tijuana eating barbequed iguana . . ." Getting lost in the music, singing, and acting goofy helped us to forget even for just a little while. It seemed as though Mark spoke to us through the lyrics of his favorite musicians. Two new songs by U2 made me cry, "The Sweetest Thing" and "New Year's Day." As did a new one by New Radicals, "You've Got the Music in You." But of all the music on the radio, there is one song that I refuse to listen to—"Angel" by Sarah McLachlan. It brings me to tears whenever

Chapter Three: The Morning After

I hear it. If that song plays on the radio, I'll change the station instantly. If it plays while I'm driving, I'll—just barely avoiding a major car accident—lunge for the tuning dial and smack and hit it hysterically until I don't hear it anymore. If I'm in a public place and hear it play overhead, I'll leave. I even forbid the children to listen to it in my presence. If they forget, they know that I'll turn into an insane maniac, cover my ears, and yell "Change it! Change it!" until they do.

Christmas was fast approaching. Knowing that Mark's gifts were in the trunk of my car was like having an elephant riding in my backseat. Thankfully, my best friend returned them for me. As much as I wanted to, I couldn't get into the holiday spirit not even for the children's sake. There wasn't going to be any annual ritual of cookie making or house decorating or a visit to the tree farmer and his wife. So much for New Year's resolutions, I might as well have just thrown 1998's calendar into the recycle bin. But I couldn't. I would always treasure the events of our last year together. With the best of intentions, Mark's sister brought us a tree and hung an angel ornament on it. But even that didn't do it for me. It just would be Christmas without Mark.

A few days shy of the holiday, the children and I were woken up early by voices in the house. Sleepily, I wrapped a robe around myself and went to investigate. I was shocked by what I witnessed. It wasn't Santa paying us an early visit, but Mark's brother and Mark's boys busily packing and taking whatever they thought was rightfully theirs from the house. I stood among them. As if I were invisible, not one of them said a word to me. They seemed to look right through me and yet not at all. A cold breeze swept over me. I looked around and noticed that all of the doors were wide open, letting out the precious heat and allowing the December cold to come in. My polite request for them to close the doors went upon deaf ears. They replied simply that they wouldn't be there much longer. Confused and feeling awkward, I walked back to the bedroom and shut the door. I crawled back into the bed and snuggled next to the children. It wasn't long before the cold seeped under the door and under the blankets. Huddling even closer together for warmth, we waited for our visitors to leave. Just as Lexi's teeth began to chatter and her little body began to shake, the disconnected heater that the bed was up against suddenly blazed a big burning red of instant warmth. We all jumped off the bed quickly and moved it away from the wall. And just as swiftly, we returned to the warmth underneath the covers. Oblivious to the miracle that just occurred, the children cuddled even deeper into the cozy folds and instantly fell back to sleep. I curled up next to them. I could never share what just happened with anyone. No one would ever believe me. Comforted by the thought that Mark's love and support was still with us, tears wet my pillow, and I eventually drifted to sleep.

We awoke a little while later to a cold and nearly empty house. The TV and stereo were gone as well as all of the boys' belongings, and furniture had been moved around. It looked as though we had been robbed. Like the wrath of a hurricane, they left a mess in their wake. I couldn't believe it. I did my best to explain to the children what happened, but it didn't help. They wanted to watch cartoons. Later that afternoon, Mark's sister stopped by to visit. She was visibly upset when she arrived. In so many words, she said that the children and I would not be allowed to *stay* there anymore. Her words seemed to float in the air. I couldn't comprehend what she meant. None of it made sense. I couldn't digest it; first Mark, now this? Not only were we facing excision from the family we thought we were a part of, but we also were going to be evicted from our home as well? She defended herself by adding that she hadn't played a part in the decision. It had been decided by the rest of the family. I was told it was because I had been laid off my job and that they couldn't afford to provide for me and the children until I regained employment. She said that they were coming the following morning to evict us and that she wanted to tell me so we wouldn't be surprised. She said she was instructed to help me pack, to assure that we didn't take any of Mark's things. In disbelief and in my defense, I explained that what we had of our own wasn't much more than personal belongings as we had done away with a lot of our things when we moved in. I pleaded with her to understand and not force us to leave with nothing especially at Christmas.

After a moment, with consideration of the situation we both faced, she said that although she had the family's trust, she would allow me to take whatever necessities we needed that I could fit into my car. I wanted to hug her for the mercy she showed me and the children, but I hesitated. Inwardly, I doubted her loyalty. I wondered just how genuine her concern for us really was and if I would ever trust her or anyone in Mark's family again. I insulated my feelings by staying focused on the urgency of all I had to do. But that only lasted for so long. Soon the numbness wore off, and the shock of what was about to happen to us began to set in. I choked back tears as I thought of how I should be wrapping presents rather than packing. *Where would we go?* I asked myself. We couldn't stay with my mom because she lived in subsidized housing; she would risk eviction. We couldn't go to my sister's as she was also a struggling single mom, and even with the best of intentions, we'd end up killing each other after just a couple of days.

As I worked at the task at hand, a neighbor stopped by to visit. She was surprised to see that I was packing. In a zombie-like stupor, without taking my eyes off what I was doing, I explained the current schedule of events. So absorbed in my thoughts and the daunting task before me, I didn't notice when she left. While I sorted through the linen closet and the kitchen, his sister went to the store and brought back some boxes. All that the children and I now owned fit into just a few of them. I saw concern on the children's faces. To put them at ease, I made up an adventure story as an explanation why we were leaving, but they didn't buy it especially because tears rolled down my face as I told it. With the backseat folded down, we stuffed the tiny coupe as full as we could, leaving just enough room for the children and me. The children cried when it was time to say goodbye to Mark's sister. The neighbor, who stopped by earlier, returned just as we were getting into the car. She handed me a piece of paper with an address written on it. She said that the children and I could stay there as long as we needed. She whispered in my ear, as she hugged me, "It's going to be okay. Be strong. The children need you." Speechless and near tears, I nodded. I hugged her in return and thanked her. I put on a brave face for the children's sake, but inside I was scared to death. With empty pockets and heavy hearts in the middle of a cold December's night, like exiled refugees, we reluctantly left our home—our happy ever after—and Omar, Cinder-Mamma kitty, Dinky, and Amos. Only looking forward, we drove toward an uncertain future.

Chapter Four: The Journey Begins

Amazing Grace

Amazing grace, how sweet the sound,
That saved a wretch like me . . .
I once was lost but now am found,
Was blind, but now I see.
T'was grace that taught . . . my heart to fear.
And grace, my fears relieved,
How precious did that grace appear . . .
The hour I first believed.
Through many dangers, toils, and snares . . .
I have already come.
T'was grace that brought me safe thus far . . .
And Grace will lead me home.
The Lord has promised good to me . . .
His word my hope secures.
He will my shield and portion be . . .
As long as life endures.
Yes, when this flesh and heart shall fail,
And mortal life shall cease;
I shall possess, within the veil,
A life of joy and peace.
The earth shall dissolve like snow,
The sun forbear to shine;
But, God, who called me here below,
Will be forever mine.
When we've been here ten thousand years . . .
Bright shining as the sun.
We've no less days to sing God's praise . . .
Then when we first begun.
Amazing Grace, how sweet the sound, that saved a wretch like
me . . .
I once was lost but now am found,
Was blind, but now, I see.

Back to the Alley

I followed the directions on the piece of paper. I pulled into a parking lot adjacent to the destination. I looked at the note more closely. I was certain the address was written incorrectly. We were not at someone's home. We were at the grandest hotel in Lynnwood, the Embassy Suites! After checking the address again, there was no doubt about it; it was the address we were given. We stared in awe at the building's magnificence. We couldn't have asked for a better Christmas gift. Even grander was the lobby where the children and I were greeted with open arms and condolences. I was given the key to room 231. We were invited to stay as long as we needed, that breakfast was complimentary, but we would have to provide our own lunch and dinner. When I opened the door to our room and saw the extravagance that awaited us, tears fell from my eyes. The room was exactly the type that Mark would have picked for us: luxurious furnishings, elegant wallpaper and decorations, table lamps with soft light to give it a tranquil ambiance, a private bedroom, a living room, a minikitchen with a little refrigerator, and a spacious bathroom. I couldn't believe it. Not in a million years could I believe this. Dale went straight for the TV and set about preparing it for his video games. Lex ran straight to the single bedroom and jumped up and down on top of one of the two big cushy queen-size beds.

I gathered the children to sit with me on the couch. They listened carefully as I explained the rules expected as guests at the hotel. And if we wanted to stay, we had to be very quiet like ghosts. We walked back to the car to park closer to the building and brought in some of our belongings. It was close to midnight by the time we finished getting ready for bed. Lex and I shared one bed, and Dale had the other one to himself. Once tucked in, I read them a story and turned off the lights. Nearly asleep, I heard Lexi cry silently to herself. I gathered her into my arms and asked her what the matter was. She said that she missed Daddy Mark. Dale whispered that he did too. Desperate for a Band-Aid to patch their little broken hearts, I told them how I once read that if we spoke out loud to him, he could hear us. Lexi's sobbing stopped immediately as she contemplated this possibility. And then they began to speak at once. Dale paused and reluctantly agreed to let her go first. She rattled on and on, telling Daddy Mark everything and anything. When it was Dale's turn, he spoke very little. He fought back tears as he tried to speak. My heart ached for both of them more than it already did and even more so with the realization that there wasn't anything I could do about it. After they each had their say and were snuggled into their beds once again, Lex interrupted the silence to ask me how we would know if he was really there. Baffled even more by this question, I suggested that she ask out loud if he was really there.

So she did.

Suddenly a loud cracking sound came from the corner of the room. *Great*, I thought to myself; now she was wide-awake and as excited as if it was Christmas Day. "He's here! He's here!" she yelled as she jumped up and down on the bed and clapped her hands in amusement. Dale joined in. "Dad, are you really here?" A loud crack sounded from another area of the room. Lex squealed in delight. I felt a little spooked by what was occurring. So playing along to make them stop their little game, I told them that maybe Dad was telling them to go to sleep. Their silliness instantly ceased, and they hurriedly scrambled underneath their covers. "Good night, Daddy," Lex said just before she—finally—fell sound asleep. I laid awake a while more thinking as they slept. Comforted by the familiar dark shadow even in the corner of this strange room, I turned away from it to face the wall and soon fell fast asleep myself. And while I slept, I had the strangest dream. I dreamt that I wrote a book from its beginning to end. I saw everything vividly: the photo for the book cover, the title and its placement on the cover, the format of the contents, the main text, and the index—everything about the book was given to me in this dream. I was to write this story to help other survivors of tragic loss. It was so imprinted in my mind that I would never forget it.

I awoke before the children to have a peaceful shower. I stumbled into the bathroom and was shocked by the reflection in the mirror. I didn't recognize the person staring back at me. *Where did she go?* I asked myself. No wonder the kids seemed afraid of me. I washed my face, but the haunting image remained the same. The dream took forefront as I showered. I couldn't fathom how one went about writing a book. A person, most certainly, would require a college degree to produce one so I immediately put the thought of it out of my mind. I made the effort to put on some makeup and reevaluated my reflection. There wasn't any change. Grief aside, I called Barry. He was dumbfounded by our situation but assured me that we would be all right and that he would research our options. He called later that afternoon with bad news. The law didn't recognize Mark and I as legally married nor were we considered married by common law. Therefore, the children and I would not be entitled to Mark's pension, social security, or any of the funds donated by the public. I nearly dropped the phone. I couldn't believe it. I hung up with a defeated "goodbye" and went into the bathroom and shut the door. I sat on the edge of the bathtub—besot by the irony in my life—shoved my face deep into a soft and luxurious hotel towel, and cried the makeup away.

Thankfully, the children were on winter break so we didn't have to worry about school for a while. Breakfast at the hotel was something we always looked forward to. We'd stuff ourselves to the gills, and like chipmunks, we harbored enough food from the buffet bar to our room to last us through dinner. The following day, I called the local social service office to learn that we were not eligible for any type of assistance. According to their charts, I made too much money in former months to qualify. Discouraged but not defeated, I forged on in search of other options. Thankfully, it turned out that I was eligible for unemployment benefits.

Regrettably though, the money wasn't available for another two weeks, and it wouldn't be very much, but it was better than nothing. I worried how we would manage. In the meantime, I was given an appointment to see a social worker for employment assistance. The day of the appointment, I hesitated as I put my hand out to introduce myself. As an unwilling participant on the newly appointed path of my life, I decided that I didn't want to be known as Lis anymore. If I had to start my life over, then my name would change too. So I introduced myself by a shortened version of my given name—one that Lexi's teacher addressed me by—Elise. Within two weeks, I acquired some job leads and enrolled the kids for medical benefits. To tide us over until the unemployment funds came, I found several area food banks and the times that they were open.

Visiting hours were the only written rules for the food banks. We figured out the assumed ones the hard way. After waiting for what seemed an eternity in the freezing cold and pouring rain, we learned that the lines formed early, the dairy products went first, and dressing for inclement weather was imperative. With our rations in hand, I picked through them selectively and kept only what we needed as the refrigerator at the hotel and the trunk of my car could only store so much. The remaining food I brought to my mom and the tenants who lived in her building. Although the food was mostly processed or canned, it kept us alive; and for that, I was especially grateful. In my heart, I knew that it wouldn't always be this way. The children were beside themselves; they couldn't believe their luck. "Cookies and SpaghettiOs!" Winter break soon ended, and the children were back in school. Because we no longer lived by the school bus stop, I had to drive them back and forth each day. While they were away—although I would rather have climbed back into bed and hid away from the world—I spent the long hours searching tirelessly for solutions out of the mess that I had gotten us into. I went to appointments, ran errands, applied for available jobs, and made time to visit Mark. My first visit was unnerving. Although I purposely made a mental note of the surroundings and the landmarks where he lay exactly the day of the funeral, it still took me forever to find him.

Chapter Four: The Journey Begins

Freshly dug earth and a barely visible burial tag were the only indicators of his resting place. I draped my coat carefully onto the ground under which he was buried. I knelt down and pressed my cheek firmly to the cold, damp earth. I wanted to be as close to him as I possibly could. Lying on my stomach, I closed my eyes and stretched out my arms to embrace his grave. I gripped the newly seeded soil with each of my hands. I let my fingers sink as deeply as they could into the silky softness, hoping to reach deep enough to touch him, and cried. While I lay there, like tears from heaven, the sky opened up; and the rain poured down. I welcomed it—the water falling out of the sky—the dark and gloominess of it all. It seemed as though Mark was crying with me. I ignored the ever-increasing dampness of my clothing and my hair. I kept my eyes closed and continued to whisper to him. I told him how much we missed him and what was happening with us. Regaining some common sense and composure, I sat up on my knees, bent down, and kissed his tiny marker ever so tenderly and sweetly. I wiped the dirt from my hands and the tears from my face. I gathered my coat and reluctantly left Mark behind as I headed back to the hotel.

Whenever I visited Mark's grave, I'd leave a memento like a laminated picture of us or some flowers. But when I returned the following week, the gifts would be gone. I was devastated when the minipotted Christmas tree that the children and I lovingly decorated for him mysteriously disappeared. I couldn't understand why only ours was taken. Other gifts had remained, as did other gifts on other graves, but not ours. No matter though, I knew, in my heart, that the one thing no one could ever take away from us was Mark's love. Undaunted, I decided to leave secret mementos, the tiniest and most insignificant gestures of love and tuck them in and around his grave: a button from my blouse, a ribbon from Lex, and a small piece of all our hair. One would have to know that they were there to find them. And so, with each visit thereafter, a justified feeling would calm my anxious heart once I discovered our gifts remained untouched.

Like a ghost from the past, Lexi's biological father resurfaced. With much discussion, it was decided that it would be best for her to stay with him and his wife until I was back on my feet. In the meanwhile, Lex would visit me on weekends. They lived in Lacey—it might as well have been in New York. The day I gave her away was yet another one of the *worst days of my life*. But wanting her home, wanting us all together, and wanting stability for all of us again gave me even more determination to get through each new day that didn't have Mark's love and encouragement in it.

It wasn't long before a coworker from my former employer found us at the hotel. She wanted to bring me a gift. I was glad to see her again and to receive the hug she gave me. She handed me a card. I was moved by the many heartfelt condolences written inside. There was also a letter. It was from the hospital. They had formed a donation fund for me and my children. While I struggled for the right words to say, she presented yet another gift. It was a beautiful piece of translucent beveled crystal glass; and pressed in its center, held forever in eternity, was some of the last flowers Mark gave me. I cried as I remembered the day he brought Safeway flowers to my office—the day before he died. The priceless keepsake was sealed with gold-colored lead. I was speechless. It was the most unique and sentimental gift I had ever received. Words could never express my gratitude. And as if that still wasn't enough, she surprised me even further by offering her home to us, insisting that we come to stay with her and her family.

A New Beginning

$\mathcal{D}$ale and I gladly moved in with her. We were given the guest bedroom and invited to stay as long as we needed. It was nearly as large as the hotel room. It had two full-size beds and a bathroom. They were the most gracious hosts. They shared all they had with us. Thankfully, the weekends came quickly, bringing Lex home with us once again. Continuing with their nighttime ritual, the children listened intently for Mark's familiar *noises* before they would go to sleep. He never failed them. But for me, nighttime continued to be the worse. I was held captive by my worries and concerns and unable to run away from them as I did during the day. On one particular sleepless night, as I buried my face into my pillow to stifle my frustrated cries, I felt a warm heaviness of someone sitting next me. I reached my hand out, in the darkness, to let whoever it was know that I was all right; but there wasn't anyone there. Confused, I turned to see where they were. Oddly enough, I didn't see anyone there, yet I still felt someone sitting next to me—there was even an indention in the bed. Unafraid, feeling even more saddened and alone, I rolled back over, stuffed my face into the pillow, and continued to cry. Gradually, the warmth moved from beside me to the length of my back and across my arms, the same way Mark used to hold me to sleep at night. No matter which way I tossed or turned, rubbed at my arms, or moved my legs, the warmth remained. My restlessness finally calmed. Comforted, I soon fell fast asleep.

Running away from my feelings was becoming second nature to me. Aware of the fact that my friend worked with doctors who specialized in grief made me feel self-conscious and uncomfortable around her. The new rationalizations of how I viewed the world seemed only to make sense to me. Although she wanted to be close, I just wanted to be left alone. I know she just wanted to help, but I wasn't ready to listen. So like the Gingerbread man, I eventually pushed her away along with everyone else including my best friend and, eventually, myself. I purposely avoided everyone. I didn't want to be touched or to feel the comfort of a well-meaning hug, and I most definitely did not want to hear the dreaded words of condolence. It only reminded me that I wasn't in a coma and that Mark was really gone. I subconsciously made enemies of anyone who ever suggested that I celebrate Mark's life rather than consume myself in the sorrow of his death, or that I move on or forward, or that it was better to have loved than to never have loved at all. I didn't expect anyone to understand how I felt, rational or otherwise. I felt smothered by their attempts to make it *better*. Without Mark, I felt void inside. Somehow, I had let my ultimate happiness be defined by Mark's very existence. I had unwittingly lost my sense of self-worth. Gradually, I turned inward and isolated myself more and more from the *real* world. And along the way, I lost the sound of the wind blowing, the rain falling, and the birds singing.

I applied for an office assistant job with King County. They called me in for a job interview and then again for a second one. I was excited the day I got the job. I found it difficult to concentrate and process like I used to, but I started with small tasks and gradually took on more and more, learning new skills in the process. Thankfully, it wasn't stressful, and everyone was friendly. By the third month of the 1999's new year, I could afford to move into an apartment. The apartment was next to the park and ride where I took the bus to work every day. It felt awkward at first, a full circle since the last time I parked there on that fateful day. It seemed less nerving to ride on a Community Transit bus rather than on a Metro. I gradually adjusted to the occasional compassionate stares from strangers. Sometimes, I smiled back at them to reassure them that I was all right even though I wasn't.

Going back and forth to work each day, I noticed how the world seemed to continue as if nothing had happened. Everyone seemed to be happy, to have goals and a purpose. I found myself constantly faced with *reminders*: a metro bus—exactly like the last one Mark drove—a metro driver, Mark's friends, and tons of Pooh and Piglet stuff. It affected my mood and mental attitude. If I didn't have children to provide for, I would have ran screaming all the way back home. I began to collect my own reminders. In a manic frenzy, I collected everything and anything related to Mark and the day of the tragedy. I collected anything that would provide evidence of his existence—media, transcription, pictures, condolence cards, gifts, etc. Like a time capsule, unopened and unread, I kept all of the things—and my conviction that *it* really didn't happen—inside of a large Rubbermaid storage container. And like a ball and chain, I never let that box be far from me. Although I refused to deal with its contents, I coveted it just the same.

The apartment was just a little bigger than the hotel, but it was a start. With what little belongings we had, it seemed just right. I brought my mom to stay with us for a few days. She helped as she could and kept the children entertained. And even here, just as the children were tucked into their beds at night, the unexplainable yet not so unusual noises continued in every corner of the room upon their beckoning. As for me, I knew I could count on the familiar warmth to console me to sleep. With everything coming together, I decided that it was time for Lex to come home for good. But her father wouldn't give her back without a fight. With legal assistance, I won her back but with a price of $2,000 for child support during the brief time that she lived with them even though he owed me much more. To make matters worse, he said that if I wanted her, I had to go and get her—eighty miles to Lacey. With limited driving experience, the thought of driving to Lacey scared me to death. But the love for my baby superseded that fear and gave me the determination needed to bring her home.

I began the journey after work, on a Friday, from the park and ride. All was well until the sun went down, and the dark settled in, bringing with it a menacing wind. It whipped around my car and nearly jerked it out of the lane. Then a monsoon began to fall in one constant shower. Because the windshield on my car was slanted, using the wipers proved futile. Even on the highest setting, they couldn't wipe the rain away fast enough. I sat up as close as I could to the windshield but still couldn't see a thing. I felt as if I were in a toy boat washed away at sea. My knuckles blanched white and my arms became numb as I fought with the steering wheel to keep the car in one lane. I started to cry. I attempted to wipe away the tears with the back of my hand but inevitably smeared the mess across my face, making the visibility even worse. In fear and frustration, I cried out to Mark. And just when I thought I was going to lose the battle, the exit sign to Lacey was illuminated before me. Relieved, I took the first deep breath since my journey began and exited off the highway from hell. I turned into the gas station where Lex and her father waited for me. Exhausted, my shirt drenched with perspiration, I wiped the sticky spider-webbed mess off my face with some napkins that I found in my purse and climbed out of my car. Lex ran to me. Too drained to have words with her father, I gathered her victoriously into my arms and headed back toward the dreaded interstate. Thankfully, the storm had passed. Lexi—being her mother's daughter—knew just how to cheer me up. She tuned the radio to our favorite country station, and we caterwauled to the tops of our lungs all the way back home.

All was complete with Lex home. I continued to visit Mark's grave and brought the children if they wanted to go. It became customary to bring tiny mementos as tokens of our love and to hide them in and around his grave. With my new job and the children busy with all sorts of activities, our visits became fewer and shorter; and eventually, we visited only on special occasions. Life was easier to manage when I stayed busy. So I participated when and where I could and jumped on every opportunity that provided another reason for me to be even busier. Being on copilot and going through the motions of everyday life was the easiest way for me not to think about *it*. There were still some though who continued to hold their breath, waiting for the other shoe to drop. I had no idea when and if I'd ever feel like my old self again. I became lost within my inner turmoil. I became nonexistent and lost track of time. Thankfully, the children continued to thrive and push on ahead without all of me present. Sadly though, I missed out on the joys of their last years of childhood.

Coping

To protect myself from the feelings that I couldn't deal with, I subconsciously created new battles for myself. One in particular I fought with constantly was the need to be in control of my immediate environment. I avoided obsessively anything and everything that brought up *those* feelings namely all parks and towns anywhere near *ground zero*. So poof! One day, they just didn't exist. No more Woodland Park Zoo, Greenlake, Freemont, or any of those places—all gone. And to make doubly sure that I didn't happen by those areas, I vowed to never ride, as a passenger, in anyone else's vehicle. I couldn't trust that they wouldn't take me there for my own good. As well, I became more and more over vigilant and over concerned with my children and everything else in my life. In my heart, I felt a very real and overwhelming sense of dread that if I didn't fiercely protect all that I held dear, somehow I would lose it again. Ultimately, I succeeded in convincing myself that the world was not a safe place, and that—in and of itself—affected my ability to believe that anything would ever be okay again. I continued to talk to Mark, the only one I knew who would listen and understand.

With the conviction that I've always managed before and the certainty that I still could, my stubborn pride kept me from asking for the help that we needed, but somehow, it came anyway and always when we needed it the most. Most remarkably were—and continues to be—pennies from heaven: rebate checks from various bills that I had overpaid from years before, anonymous professional checks, and untraceable payments on utility bills. Even stranger, a small amount of extra money will manifest in my bank account without a transaction ever being made. In addition to our divine financial security, I had a divine copilot as well. Since Mark's death, I had been walking around in a fog of confusion and self-absorption, but I somehow still managed. Crazy as it may sound, I didn't hear voices per se, but I had *thoughts.* These *thoughts* guided me through each day from decision making to taking care of the children. And I never second guessed it, I just went along. Because the *thoughts* never pointed me in the wrong direction, I began to trust and rely on them. Everything seemed to fall into place. Most importantly, they consoled me whenever my heart felt the heaviest. With them, I never felt alone or indifferent.

With all that we had been through and what was about to be mine and Mark's official wedding day, I decided to take the children to Disneyland. It was exactly what we were in such desperate need for. It's been said that it is "the happiest place on earth." While on a break from work, I made the travel arrangements for our trip. The man who helped me made me laugh. Not so much by what he said or the sound of his voice but by the uncanny way he spoke. It was verbatim—the same quotes and phrases—in the same way that Mark would've said them. I barely remembered the way Mark spoke until that phone conversation. After the call, I cried silently to myself. A coworker came to my desk, knelt next to me, and gently put her hand on my back. Not expecting her to understand, I told her anyway of the experience I just had. Later that day, while entering some data on my computer, the background on the screen suddenly changed from black to green. I showed it to my coworker. Neither of us could explain the change. And just as suddenly, it went back to normal again. I laughed to myself, trying not to cry. Green was Mark's favorite color.

My newfound neurosis threatened to poison our trip. I organized everything down to the last minute and dollar and ran our vacation like a relay race. In spite of it all, we had a great time. The children relinquished months of pent-up emotion with every fast-moving ride they could climb on. In the evenings, they'd unwind in the hotel swimming pool. Exhausted, as soon as their little heads hit their pillows, they'd fall into a deep sleep, forgetting just for a moment and letting go for just a little bit. Watching them play, laughing, and having so much fun again

Homeless

Embassy Suites

Worker Memorial Day in Olympia, WA March 28, 1999

Governor Locke deems Mark a hero

WA State DOL annual awards ceremony

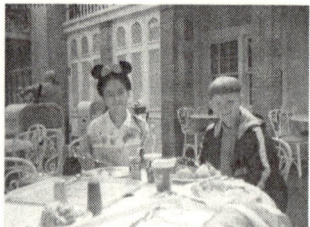

Daddy Mark is listed a hero on the Wall of Fame!

The happiest place on earth

Memorial dedication, North Base,
November 23, 1999

Bridge dedication, First
Anniversary, November 27, 1999

Barry Samet, ATU 587 president
Glen Travis, ATU 587 vice president
Ron Sims, King County executive

Bridge dedication, first anniversary, November 27, 1999

Candy canes for kids, December 1999

Together . . . Moving forward one day at a time

Lucky

was exactly the purpose of the trip. We took a lot of great pictures and brought home a handful of treasures. Upon our arrival home, I received a letter from the Department of Labor and Industry. We were invited to a memorial ceremony to honor Mark and other Washington State workers who died in the line of duty in 1998. The children and I, Barry, and some other drivers drove to Olympia on an unassigned Metro bus with Mark's ID number, 2106, illuminated on the directional sign. It was a beautiful, honorable, and memorable service. Each worker's name was written in a special book, along with others before them, and encased in a permanent display. As well, Governor Gary Locke officially deemed Mark a hero for his efforts to save so many lives with just his last breath on that fateful day.

Commuting back to work, I noticed a book that an acquaintance was reading—*Talking to Heaven* by James van Praagh. She told me as much as she could about the book before we arrived at our designated stop. She gave me her business card. The name Ralph and a phone number were written on the back of it. She said that he, like the author of her book, was a local medium whom she sought guidance from for many years.

Ralph

Out of curiosity—mostly because Mark had talked about these kinds of things—I called the number as soon as I arrived home and made an appointment. On the day of the appointment, I was surprised that my directions brought me to a gift shop. I looked at the address on the paper. I was certain I was in the right place. A clerk noticed my uncertainty. Without any questions, he guided me toward the back of the store, up a short flight of stairs, and into a large and dimly lit room. It was permeated by the smell of incense. Candle wax dripped ever so slowly from candles placed strategically around the room, and a parrot cackled somewhere in the background.

I was seated across an enormously large man. I felt more skeptical than afraid. He began by placing a cassette into a tape recorder. I said very little, if not nothing at all, to test his authenticity. In a friendly and heavy-English accent, he told me things that I wouldn't understand until much later, until I had mostly forgotten my visit and the predictions he made that day. He asked about a ring. He said he could see it upside down and asked if I had recently become single. Not wanting to give him any cues and mostly wanting to know about Mark, I tucked my hand—with the ring on it—under my leg and masked my emotions as best as I could. It was challenging to follow his ramblings and mumblings that sometimes went on and on and around and around in no particular sequence. In this odd place, I really felt like I was in wonderland and that I was visiting with a real life Mad Hatter.

He told me that everything around me was really weird at the moment. He said that he could still see the ring, like a wedding ring, and that it was turning around and around but not broken. He felt that the relationship had ended. He said that there was something about me and this relationship that wasn't sorted out though. He said there was life still in this relationship and that it seemed to be on pause. He stopped for a moment and shook his head. With a sense of shock in his voice, he asked if the man had left me. Muttering to himself, as if trying to unravel a mystery, he said that the strangest thing was that—although this man was away—he had a sense that he was standing right next to me. Nodding to himself with firm assurance, he asked if the man had passed away.

Shifting his thoughts and continuing to mutter in no particular sequence, he said, "When you are in bed at night and you get the feeling he's there, he wants you to know that he really is there. Though he is not with you every second of the day, he truly misses you as much as you miss him. What we have here are two people in a terrible situation. It is going to take some time, but it is something that you will be able to work through. He still finds that he needs to be around you and, that at the times when you're distracted but suddenly think of him for no reason, do not to feel down because it's at those times he's checking on you." Switching gears again, he said, "He has been trying to show you that he is with you by tilting pictures, hiding your keys, etc." Pausing briefly, seemingly lost in his thoughts but with happiness in his voice, he uttered to no one in particular, "It sure was a lovely ring." Then from out of nowhere, he said, "I'm getting the word *shithead*." I burst out laughing; now I was certain that Mark was with us. He paused again, shaking his head, as a look of deep-felt sadness came over his face. He asked if he had died a sudden death.

He said, "I get the feeling that although it was sudden, it seems as though it was predestined—a prearranged thing. As if it was his time to go though his conscience didn't know, but his soul did. The adjustment is going to be difficult for both of you because there is work still to do. But you will eventually heal and move forward, some days will be easier than others." Distracted for a moment, he continued, "You will live to be quite old because you have many things still to do." He stopped abruptly and muttered something about my eyes. He asked if my eyes were what he was first attracted to. Strangely, the first song Mark had played for me by U2, "I Will Follow," entered my thoughts; and I lost it. Great, I had done it now. I just gave this guy the lead he needed to continue. But I couldn't help myself; some of the things he said were too coincidental. In my heart, I wanted to believe. Mark talked a lot about my eyes. He loved my eyes and always commented that they were hypnotic like a mermaid's siren—just like the blue stone in my ring. As usual, once I began to unravel, it was nearly impossible to regain composure. I sniffled to myself as Ralph continued.

He asked, "Have you been having dreams about visiting with him? They aren't dreams. You need to keep a journal of his visits. He needs you as much as you need him." Ralph went on to describe Mark's personality and mine as well. He said that I always made Mark laugh, and I had made him feel good about himself. He described my future and said many great things were going to happen to me. Ironically, he told me not to worry about money. With surprise in his voice, ricocheting his thoughts once more, he exclaimed, "He loves children doesn't he?" With even more surprise, he asked if I was a mother; and before I could respond, he nodded his head in conviction and said that I had had two pregnancies and then asked to see my hand.

Chapter Four: The Journey Begins

Looking seriously into my palm, he interpreted the lines there. Surprised, he asked if I had been married before because I had a broken line. Changing the subject, he went on to say, "What a great mom you are. You have the mind of an adult as well as that of a child. Your children will be fine. You will always make things fun for them, they will never lack in love, and they will not end up drug addicts or have any serious problems." Zigzagging his thoughts, he said, "You will never look your age, and this will piss off a lot of women around your own age. You have an extremely full life ahead of you. And although you are a very independent lady and could never be accused of being easy, men will continue to hit on you. And although you will never show any interest, you will definitely marry again." He paused, as if listening to something, and then muttered, "Martin." Asking aloud who this was, he said the name again. "Oh Martin!" Muttering again, shaking his head with utmost certainty, he said, "It's either part of his first or last name." After a moment, he exclaimed, with even more certainty, "It is most definitely a part of his last name!" Confused, I asked whose last name he was referring to. He said matter-of-factly, "It is the name of the man you will marry someday, but not for a long while."

He concluded our visit by telling me that my present journey would be difficult, but I wouldn't be walking it alone. I had a lot of spirits around me, helping me to heal and cope, and that they would remain with me until I didn't need them as much anymore. He said that I was very well protected and that my intuition level was high. And when someone with this high level gets an emotional hurt, it's devastating—the worst—but the guides would help me through it. He affirmed that there wouldn't be anymore big disasters ahead of me. He said some people would be helpful, and others would gradually drift away because they wouldn't know what to say to me. He popped the cassette out of the player and handed it to me and exclaimed how wonderful it was to meet me. I hugged him in return and thanked him for his time. Arriving home, I carefully wrapped the cassette in tissue paper and put it into Mark's box. I regarded the experience as no more than a grain of salt and eventually forgot all about it.

One Foot In Front of the Other

*N*ext on the to-do list was to find a permanent home for us. It wasn't long before I found a three-bedroom townhouse on the corner of a private cul-de-sac in Mukilteo. There were quite a few hurdles I had to clear before I could get it because I didn't have a credit history. One of which was to sell my new car. I traded it in for a used and more affordable Geo Storm. When all was said and done, the house was ours. I spent many sleepless nights fixing it up. We moved in just before the start of a new school year and threw a house-warming party with some friends and coworkers. Even with so much to celebrate, my heart still felt heavy. Guilt ate at my insides for not feeling entirely exuberant for what we acquired thus far. We had come such a long way since the hotel. But I didn't want all of these new things, these new changes. All I wanted was to be home with Mark, in our home, among the things that we had made a life out of.

Wanting to feel *better*, tired of the grey cloud that hung constantly over my head, I set out on a mission to find some sort of instruction manual to manage this unfair rite of passage in my life. I wanted to know exactly how I was supposed to feel, how I was supposed to act, and what was *normal*. I wanted to have the answers that my children so desperately sought. I needed something in stone, black-and-white—something that didn't require too much thinking. I was certain there was something written out there. Driven, I researched tirelessly through tons of literature and articles on grief but didn't relate to any of them. I searched desperately for answers but was never satisfied with what I found. Unable to find a magical "how to" manual, I felt defeated and lost. Even more depressing was the realization that I couldn't lead my children when I couldn't even find my own way. I didn't know what to do. I didn't know how to do this. Ironically, the more hopeless it all seemed, the more I dreamt about *the book*. But once again,

Chapter Four: The Journey Begins

I ignored the dream. I paid little or no attention to its message, but the dream continued. Like everything else, I put it on a back burner in the farthest corner of my mind. I knew I couldn't write my story if I hadn't been through the process myself and that was a journey I was none too eager to begin.

Settling into our new home was quite an adjustment. With what little belongings we had, the house—with its tall ceilings and vast spaciousness—felt cold and empty. Because we were used to sleeping within a stone's throw from each other and because Dale had the bigger bed, we camped out in his room for the first month. Even though the children no longer sought the assurance of Mark's presence before they fell asleep at night, a crack or two from the walls and ceilings stilled echoed a silent lullaby throughout the slumbering quietness of the house. Sadly, the enveloping warmth that I relied upon to sooth me asleep gradually faded away too. In its place were endless nights of tossing and turning, worrying and longing for Mark and for what once was.

Barry and I occasionally met at the County building for lunch. Keeping on the surface, I told him how my life was going, and he spoke about the security changes happening at Metro. He said a new Transit Security Program had been formed, how off-duty Seattle police officers patrolled the buses, and that security cameras were installed on every coach. Selfishly, I couldn't help think how much hindsight was twenty-twenty. Incredibly, Mark's forty-fifth and Lex's tenth birthday was upon us. I placed a single red rose on Mark's grave and kissed his newly placed gravestone. I threw a surprise birthday party for Lex. From an outsider's point of view, everything seemed as if it were on its way back to normal.

Soon Lex and Dale went away for two weeks to a YMCA summer camp. I was beside myself. I wasn't ready to be entirely alone. I tried to enjoy the time I had to myself, but my thoughts made it impossible. I couldn't sit still long enough to sew, and I definitely couldn't concentrate on a book. So I reached out to my mother, the one person whom I knew needed the expendable energy I wished to exhaust. I spent every moment of those two weeks happily—running errands, cleaning, and cooking for her. She even enticed me into a few games of dice. Thankfully, the time passed by quickly, and the children were home once again just in time for another letter from Metro. It was an invitation to the annual recognition and awards ceremonies of Washington State's Department of Transportation to celebrate Mark's heroism and to enter his name onto their Wall of Fame. The ceremonies were in Spokane. The kids were excited about the trip: another airplane ride, another hotel, and another swimming pool. We left on a Tuesday and returned the following day.

Incredulously, the first anniversary was upon us. Barry held a memorial at the site of the tragedy. Many of Metro workers, union leaders, transit operators, Metro's general manager, and the King County executive Ron Sims were among those who gathered there to remember Mark, to reconcile his memory, and to honor the operators who continued to provide service to the county citizens. Dale attended as well as many of Mark's family members. Lex and I stayed home. I didn't want everyone to see how well I wasn't doing, and mostly I wasn't ready to face the reality of the bridge. At the closing of the ceremony, a memorial plaque was unveiled. It was dedicated to Mark's memory, to honor his heroism on that fateful day. It was permanently attached to the pillar, at the point where Mark's bus impacted, so that his heroic efforts would never be forgotten. Within the same week, Barry arranged a memorial dedication ceremony at North Base. Another memorial plaque was unveiled. This one would be placed in the base's courtyard. Inside of a glass showcase in the foyer was a display to honor and commemorate Mark's achievements and awards since becoming a Metro employee. Unable to attend, I gathered together the many Safe Driver Award badges and pins that Mark earned over the years and arranged them chronologically inside a shadow box. Barry placed it front and center inside of the showcase.

With the anniversary came an extraordinary request from Lexi. I presented her wish to Barry. Understanding the importance behind it, he presented the idea to Metro's operating manager who spoke with the Red Cross and the Spangler Candy

Company in Bryan, Ohio. Astonishingly, the candy company donated twenty-five thousand candy canes to Metro in memory of Mark. And not the usual red-and-white striped type but the unusually flavored kind that Mark liked to hand out to all the children passengers at Christmas time. And even more amazing, a trucking company, Dawes Transport, transported all fifty-eight cases of the candy canes across the country, in blizzard-like conditions, for free! I couldn't believe how it all came together. Lex was beside herself. Just two weeks before Christmas, while the candy canes made their way west, the kids and I worked with Barry to make life-size posters introducing the candy cane drive to all of the transit drivers. When the posters were ready, they were propped on easels alongside a large barrel for the collection at each of the bases. For the next two weeks—in addition to the Spangler candy—candy canes poured in. When the day finally arrived, Barry invited the kids and me to ride on one of the routes to help pass them out. The excitement of it all masked our fear of the bus as we handed them out to all the kids who boarded. It was a great success—one that I hoped would continue year after year.

Two Steps Back

With the new millennium came seemingly insurmountable challenges. Our new home produced expensive heating bills and other costs that I wasn't prepared for: water, sewer, garbage, and association dues just to name a few. In addition to childcare, groceries, gas, and other expenses, I was soon way over my head. What I thought would be the best solution to my financial troubles turned out to be an even bigger nightmare of mismanagement—I acquired a couple of credit cards. They only made matters worse because I had to pay for those too. And to top everything off, the used car I bought began to have trouble, and so I traded it in for what I thought was something better. But my ignorance served me well. I was talked into an older Eddie Bauer Ford Explorer. They said it had room for the kids and all of our stuff and an adjustable front seat and steering wheel. It ate every penny I had in gas money and car insurance.

With the first anniversary of my job at the County came an all too familiar rumor of possible layoffs in our office due to an initiative that was about to pass. When Barry offered me a position at the union as a secretary that paid more than my County job, I jumped at the opportunity. I adjusted well to the fast-paced work environment and the extra bus I had to take in the mornings. But after only a few months on the job, the union had an election for new officers, and Barry wasn't reelected. Under the new regime, my job eventually went south. Furthermore, there would no longer be any further special recognition planned for Mark including the cancellation of Candy Canes for Kids the following Christmas. Lexi was devastated. There was nothing I could do to make her understand. And there it lay. With no more official power, there wasn't anything that Barry could do. Even though he quietly went on to resume his previous position as a transit operator, we continued to make time to meet for lunch.

I wasn't surprised the day I received a letter from the IRS to audit my 1998 taxes or when I began to have health problems: uncontrolled asthma, severe eczema on both of my hands, bursitis in both of my hips, internal ulcers, headaches, a weight gain of over forty pounds, and hair loss just to name a few. I reluctantly sought a doctor's care. I was informed that my heart was ill as well. He called it *broken heart syndrome*. But that wasn't all. He discovered yet another condition, brought on by genetics that could only be corrected surgically. He wrote a few prescriptions that, he assured me, would only be for short-term. Against Western medicine, I knew I had to comply for the children's sake. He adamantly insisted that I get into counseling and discussed in length plans for the impending surgery. Defeated by this news, the insurmountable bills, and the uncertainty of the future of my current employment, I concluded that the best thing to do was to sell our new home. Of the friends we made in the cul-de-sac, a single father offered to share his home with us while I recovered from my surgery. The children and I moved nearly all we had back into storage and moved into the kind neighbor's house. They were solemn but cooperative. I hated myself for disappointing the children yet again. Living with the neighbors was cramped to say the least—eight people in a living space of less than eight hundred square feet, three bedrooms, and one bathroom.

Since my mom and my sister had the same surgery without complications, I wasn't afraid of the procedure. That was until I awoke from the surgery to learn that I had been cut from hip to hip and had had a partial hysterectomy; they found cancer on my uterus and cervix. I was assured that all of the diseased tissue had been removed and that I would not require any further aggressive treatment. While I recovered and as fate would have it, I learned that I was allergic to every pain medication available. With every new drug that I tried, I would suffer another severe bout of hives and respiratory problems. Tylenol was my last and only result. But it did nothing to mask the pain. At times, it was so overwhelmingly intense and excruciating that any slight movement caused perspiration to pour from my body. The only blessing from this torture was that it blanketed the grief in my heart. It took several months to heal. My roommate was an angel in disguise. I wouldn't have been able to recover without him.

Faith

Once I had healed enough—mindful of what the doctor had suggested—I considered seeing a counselor. I knew I wasn't mentally ill or suffering from some serious psychiatric problem so I decided to test the waters by visiting with a pastor from a church that a friend of mine attended. He listened quietly as I exorcised all my thoughts, feelings, and unusual experiences right into his lap. Expended and satisfied, I was sure that he would understand and give me some sort of consecrated blessing to fix things. Indifferent to what I just shared, he asked if I believed in God and if I blamed him for what happened. I searched inwardly for an answer and remembered the years of Bible lessons Mark taught me. I said that I most definitely believed in God and that it hadn't crossed my mind to blame him. He told me how God lives inside of each one of us and that he is not some figure in the sky looking down and judging us.

He brought out a Bible and read from it. He read from Exodus 22:22, Psalms 68:5 and 146:9, Deuteronomy 10:18, and 1 Timothy 5:5—about how God takes care of the widows and the fatherless children. I couldn't help to think how unfair it was that I became a widow before I became a bride. From Job, he read how God remains with us in good times and bad; from Psalms, he read more beautiful and comforting passages. He read from Mark 9:23, John 20:27, and ironically Proverbs 3:5-6, the very same passage that I read from a poster the day *it* happened, about holding on to trust and faith. When he finished, I explained that I didn't understand why God concerned himself with me when I wasn't a Christian nor had I been raised in a church, nor had I lived a perfect or moral life. And even worse, I had always considered him some sort of urban legend like the Easter Bunny. Reassuringly, he explained that he loves us all, that we are all his children, and he knows when we need him the most—whether or not we feel like we've deserved it or asked for it. He said he believed that we had truly witnessed God's love and grace and that maybe, in some way, it was through Mark's death that I was to learn about him. We talked in length about grief, the process, and how one moves through it. He told me about the importance of prayer and of faith. He said that I could share all my worries and concerns at any time, and God would listen just as I had done with him when I first arrived. And then we prayed my first prayer together.

For several months, I followed the pastor's suggestions. I talked about Mark to anyone who would listen. What helped most were the prayers. I prayed all the time. I prayed for guidance, strength, and most of all, direction. The days that were the hardest to get through, I prayed right through them and somehow always felt better. Continuing with the doctor's orders, I sought grief counseling but found that talking about *it* made it hurt even more. In the mental health field, I earned yet another label, post-traumatic stress syndrome. I joined a bereavement group but did not find comfort in other people's pain. I wrote in journals, I took walks, and I went to a healing retreat. I even took my roommate and made a day out of visiting Mark's beloved Whidbey Island to bury a metal box with a lock of mine and Mark's hair, some of our mementos, pictures, and other things that were special to us underneath the Deception Pass Bridge. As part of my ritual, I lit a green candle and sat next to the shore with reverent thoughts of *saying goodbye* and *letting go* until the candle burned to the end of its wick. When I stood up to leave, a strange thing happened. Within arm's reach, a large white seal with grey spots popped its head out of the water and momentarily held me captive, with its big black eyes and steady gaze, before disappearing under the water again. The experience comforted me. It was the perfect commencement to the ritual. I smiled as I remembered Mark's lesson about animal spirituality and their relationship with God and with us.

I tried many other things, but they didn't seem to help. The wound in my heart was just as fresh as the day it tore apart. I was told it was because I wasn't ready for the process of *acceptance*. In my mind and in my heart, Mark wasn't really gone, and no one could convince me otherwise. I didn't want to process through grief ever. I just wanted Mark to come home. In a last ditch effort, I tried acupuncture and several antidepressants. All of which proved to be just as ineffective. Out of ideas, the doctor told me that modern medicine alone could not heal my broken heart—that time held the key for my healing. With spring came a renewed physical health and a deeper depression that worsened with every new challenge that I was confronted with. I returned to work at the union but only for a brief time before I was let go due to another initiative that passed. With my tail between my legs, I retreated once again to the all too-familiar unemployment line where even the staff knew me by my first name. I sent out numerous résumés and cover letters for various jobs but to no avail. I reapplied at the County, but they weren't hiring or rehiring. I chastised myself for moving from the security of that job. Whenever I found employment, it didn't last long. My mind seemed more and more distracted. Finding and keeping a full-time job became more and more difficult. I just couldn't function properly anymore in a work setting, with coworkers, or in the real world in general.

It wasn't long before our tiny living quarters turned into a battleground for our two families. And one day, I came home to an empty house. Our roommates suddenly and unexpectedly moved out. To make matters worse, the landlords were our roommate's parents. Thankfully, they agreed to let us stay. I signed a new contract for a reduced rent and an agreement to vacate the premises within four months. To save money, I traded in the Ford Explorer for an older MPV and retreated back to the food-bank lines. In between temporary odd jobs here and there, I spent hours sorting through our storage unit in search of expendable things to pawn off to pay the rent and other bills. It took a lot of effort to minimize the urgency of the situation I had gotten us into, yet again, and to keep up the façade of normalcy I projected to the outside world.

The Ruin of Gibraltar

With every new day that passed, it seemed more and more challenging to get out of bed. I was exhausted running from something I didn't understand. I found little joy in anything anymore. There was nothing to laugh about. The world was no longer beautiful. I was no longer beautiful. The weight of the world was upon my shoulders, and I was crumbling from beneath it. My body ached, and my legs felt like lead when I walked. I had fallen into a deep, dark pit with no way out. I felt more like Eeyore than Piglet anymore. My emotions came and went like the tide, and their intensity varied from hour to hour and day by day. When the tears started, the anguish in my heart would soon follow. Any little thing made me cry even if someone just asked how I was or say "I'm sorry for your loss." Their words would rip the scab off the wound in my heart, exposing an even more overwhelming sadness that dwelled in there. My insides felt torn away, leaving only an empty shell. I felt utterly and completely lost, discombobulated, and alone. Everything I'd worked for, aspired for, and hoped for all died with him. I kicked myself for my stupidity. There was no future—only a black empty space. No one would ever care for me the way Mark did. I felt like an orphan more than I ever had before.

All I felt was pain and sadness. All I could think about was *that day* and nothing before. I didn't want to celebrate any holiday or anyone's birthday or life in general for that matter. And the more I felt sorry for myself, the more I beat myself up for feeling the way I did. Eventually, I decided that I'd had enough and made a plan. The plan was to drive to the Aurora Bridge about one in the morning, when there would be little or no traffic, make myself drunker than a skunk with an entire bottle of vodka, and gun my car as hard as I could over the bridge—right into Mark's waiting arms. I was convinced death was the only way to relieve the overwhelming pain in my heart and the only way to be with Mark again. I became fixated with *the plan*. It clouded my judgment and reasoning. I didn't even consider my children. I believed they would be better off without my ever-increasing moments of instability. I believed my absence would spare them from being dragged down into a bottomless abyss of sadness and despair.

The night of *the plan*, I kissed and hugged Dale and Lexi more than usual as I put them to bed and waited until they were sound asleep. I pulled out the vodka from the back of a kitchen cupboard, put it in a paper bag, and crept silently out to my car. While I traveled south on the interstate toward the bridge, the *thoughts* nearly screamed for me to visit my mother before I continued. Bewildered but compliant, I pulled off at the exit toward her place. I knew she would still be up, sitting ever so peacefully in her easy chair, and totally absorbed in a Harlequin romance novel. She was quite surprised when I rang her security phone. When I reached her apartment, she was already at the door waiting for me. She knew something was wrong. As I guided her back to her chair, she repeatedly asked me what the matter was. Lost for words, struggling not to cry, I could only shake my head as the tears broke through my will to detain them. Once seated in her chair, I knelt beside her. Nervous, she lit a cigarette. As if I were seven years old again, I rested my head in the security of her lap and cried, oblivious to the suffocating smoke that swirled about my head. Seeing me cry made her cry too. With concern and desperation in her voice, she pried at me to explain the reason behind my unordinary and unexpected visit.

In between tears, I told her that I had come to say goodbye. The moment she understood my intention, shock and fear overshadowed her seemingly ageless face as she took my face into her hands. She looked me square in the eyes and pleaded with me not to even consider such a thing. Fearful, sliding from her chair, she knelt beside me and gathered me into her arms and held me as tightly as she could. She rocked me back and forth desperately and cried repeatedly, "No no no, Lissie!" I told her that I couldn't go on with the pain anymore—that it was too much. "But," she sobbed, "don't you see, I can't live without YOU! Who will take care of me? All I have is you. We all love you, Lissie! Me and the children, we need you!" With that, she cried and sobbed like I never heard her before—the same kind of animal cry that comes from deep within you when you fear something the most, the same kind of cry I had cried for Mark. Her body shook as she sobbed. Her tears soaked my hair and my face as she repeatedly kissed my cheeks. "Mommy's here, baby, you just hold on to me when you can't take it anymore. I can't fix it, but I can hold you. Please, Lissie, don't. Please don't do this thing." I scared her and hurt her, and I hated myself even more. We hugged and rocked each other for what seemed an eternity. "It's okay, Mommy. I won't. I won't. I'll keep trying, I promise." Sometime later, I left with the promise to call her when I got home.

And I did go home.

After a call to reassure her that I was home and all right, I crawled into bed with Lexi, curled up next to her, whispered that I was sorry for thinking such a thing, and silently wept myself to sleep. The next day, my sister called and invited us for movies and dinner. Unintentionally yet ironically, the movies she chose were just too eerily close for comfort: *City of Angels, What Dreams May Come,* and *The Sixth Sense.* The second movie seemed to speak to me in a sort of *in-between-the-lines* kind of way. The message was loud and clear. If I ever wanted to be with Mark again, I could never give up. I would end up in a horrible, lonely place far away from him, my family, and my children. And unlike the movie, there would be no way back. And the thought of never being able to see my children again and of possibly being stuck between two worlds and having to suffer the pain that I caused everyone for eternity was too much to fathom. *No, thanks,* I affirmed to myself. No matter how hopeless it all seemed, I chose then and there to tough it out.

Even though the last movie seemed like a scary movie, its ending was so surprising, yet was something so profound, that I bawled my eyes out. My sister was a little miffed. All she wanted to do was distract me and have fun for a while, but as usual, I cried and got all shook up instead. After watching the movies, I felt somewhat reassured that I wasn't crazy and that I wasn't alone in my feelings or experiences. Whoever wrote those movies didn't just have vivid imaginations; their inspiration could have only come from personal experience.

Beyond the Grave

I gradually saved enough money for us to move again. I found a nice duplex across the speedway, from where we currently lived, that allowed the children to stay in the same school district. It was an emotional relief to remove all of our belongings from storage, to unpack them, and to place them among our personal things again. Everything about our new home was peaceful. The second day of unpacking, I searched frantically through every single box that remained in the garage for mine and Mark's engagement picture. As I searched, I had one constant *thought*. It was in *the box*. For the first time, I stubbornly ignored it. I wasn't ready to open that box. Frustrated and exhausted, with several boxes still to go, I sat in a defeated heap and cried. I couldn't believe how much I accumulated even after all I had taken to the pawnshop. As I contemplated where it might be, the *thoughts* became even more consistent. "Okay, okay," I said out loud and reluctantly approached *the box*. I couldn't believe my eyes. Just as I opened the top, I saw the photo with Mark's burial flag. I had no idea how it got there. Relieved and spent, I removed it quickly and resealed *the box* once again. I dusted off our picture and placed it on the nightstand closest to my pillow.

Mark's presence seemed to be around me more than it had been before, and I felt guilty. I was supposed to be letting him go, letting him rest in peace, but I couldn't. I hung on to his memory with an iron fist. And that very well could have been the reason why unexplainable occurrences resurfaced. They didn't scare us. They mostly made us laugh. It wasn't uncommon to hear one of us say, "Dad's here!" But there were moments when the kids didn't think it was so funny. Like the times the children upset me because I couldn't get them to listen. Just when the veins in my forehead threatened to burst and my asthma thwarted my efforts to continue yelling, every light in the room would turn off and on repeatedly. You never saw two kids move as fast as they did when that happened. For whatever it was, it worked. And being children, you can probably figure out why their friends never asked to stay the night at our house especially a friend of Lexi's.

One day, we arrived home in time to see one of Lexi's friends running and screaming out of our house. She never visited again. Apparently, she invited herself into our house—it happened to be unlocked that day—and while she sat at the kitchen table, she said she heard a noise in the hallway and went to see if it was one of our cats. What she witnessed wasn't a cat. What she saw was a very large man standing in the doorway of my bedroom with an angry look on his face and pointing toward the front door. She described this man to me in great detail. Mark fit the description. We never mentioned Mark to her before. She wouldn't have known what he looked like because we didn't have any pictures hanging on the wall since we had recently moved in. She wouldn't have known that the way he pointed at her was exactly what he did when the children pushed him too far. He wouldn't say a word; he would just point. The look on his face and the direction of his pointing finger was all the children needed—and her too—to heed his authority. Mark was simply telling her that she didn't have permission to be there and to get out. One couldn't have asked for a better security system.

To be certain that we didn't have an electrical problem lurking in the wiring of the house, I had an electrician check it out thoroughly. Unsurprisingly, our five-year-old duplex got a clean bill of health. The children and I concluded that it could only be one thing, Daddy Mark, but we kept the premise to ourselves. Adding to the unexplainable was the occasional cloak of cold air around me. No matter what I did, I couldn't shake it. The kids were in awe of it. And one time, the cold touched Lex. I found her one morning alone in the kitchen crying. In between heartfelt sobs, she said she had been thinking of Daddy Mark when she felt something cold on her hand. And then she felt the cold on her cheek. She said she knew it was Daddy and cried even harder. And before I had a chance to react, she burst out laughing. Because she was laughing as hard as she had been crying, she could only point at me. I went to look in the bathroom mirror to see what she thought was so funny. And there it was; my long hair stood straight up just like an orangutan's. For the next half hour, we laughed as we watched my hair fluctuate with static. No matter where I moved in the house, the static remained. For whatever it was—the cold and the static—it was just like Mark to make Lex laugh her sad tears away.

But that was only the beginning of what Lex referred to as the *staticky moments*, and she and Dale watched for them vigilantly. The *staticky moments* were an instant mood lifter, and remembering how Mark loved to touch my hair and the great pleasure he took when brushing the freshly washed golden strands until they were dry was just the indicator the kids needed to know that Mark was present. Without missing a beat, the children would tell him as much as they could and as fast as they could before my hair would return to rest around my shoulders. Although the strange phenomena wouldn't make sense to anyone else—and maybe there is a rational explanation behind them—but believing that he was still with us gave us comfort, and that was all that mattered.

A Purifying Experience

*I*t wasn't long before Dale was old enough to be employed. His first job was at a veterinary clinic just on the other side of the speedway. Not long after, he approached me with a woeful tale of an unadoptable kitten because it had a chronic sinus infection. He coaxed me into seeing it. We wound up adding one more to our growing family of animals, and she became known as Sniffles. As a result of the necessary checkups for the kitten, we became friends with the doctor, Dr. Bob. He invited us one Christmas to a play at the church he attended. The children and I had never been to church before. After all the unexplainable events that had happened to us since Mark's death, we were curious and eager to learn more spiritually. Collectively, we decided to give it a try. Everyone was so welcoming, loving, and accepting. We couldn't help to want to be part of it, and before we knew it, we were adopted into a large and extended family. The children never complained about getting up early to go to the church services. In fact, more often than not, they were the ones rushing me to get to the services on time. We attended many family functions, and the kids joined the youth group. They sang at events and participated in plays. They even went on a couple of Christian missionary trips. And during the summers, they volunteered all their time and energy as counselors at the church's annual day camp for the little kids.

After attending for nearly a year, the pastor asked us if we would like to be baptized. We agreed that we would and spent the next several months preparing for it. If I made a list of the best days of my life, the day we were baptized together would be one of them. Kneeling before the pastor at the front of the church, with the congregation as witness, the children and I shared the most beautiful moment of our lives. As members of the church, we were encouraged to participate in different activities, which the children did wholeheartedly. I continued to prefer to be alone. Although I was excited about the new path we had chosen, it still wasn't enough to take away the sadness and pain that I had struggled with for so long. And I didn't want to burden anyone else with my issues. To avoid bringing attention upon myself, I participated in some group studies and volunteered to have some of them at my house, but that was the extent of it.

I was suspended in time with my grief and couldn't trust the church family—like everyone else—not to take it upon themselves to help me get *better*. I continued to hold steadfast to the certainty that Mark wasn't really gone and that one day, I would wake up and everything would be back to normal. I didn't want to hear otherwise, and I eventually drifted away from the church by securing a weekend job. The children continued their involvement for a while longer. But when Dale became wrapped up with the final requirements to graduate from high school and his job and Lex became busier with her own activities, they too faded away from the gathering. I think their eventual lack of interest was partly my fault.

Down the Rabbit Hole

*W*hat available time I had I spent attending to my mother or Mommy as my sister and I lovingly referred to her. With Mommy, I found solace. I could be myself. She never played judge or jury. Mommy was the only person—other than Mark—who truly understood, accepted, and loved me for who I was no matter what; as I did her. Sweet and delicate like the butterflies she loved so much, Mommy saw the world and everyone in it through innocent eyes. She saw only the good in others, trusted totally, and never had an unkind word to say about anyone.

Just barely into her sixties, she suffered from various lifelong disabilities and was in very poor health. As her illnesses began to affect her ability to care for herself, I gladly quit my weekend job to help her. I wasn't disappointed the day when I also lost my weekday job—a blessing in disguise—as she required more care. I worked several part-time jobs to make ends meet and to help the unemployment funds I finally qualified for stretch even farther. I worked around her schedule and somehow always finished in time to be home for the children when they returned from their day at school.

It was my ultimate goal to lessen her pain as well as my own. By channeling the Florence Nightingale within me, I hid from the truth of what had become our new reality. I worked feverishly, effortlessly, and tirelessly—exercising everything I was ever taught in nursing school. I changed her diet, enrolled her into a smoking-cessation program, and gave her daily hot baths and massages. In spite of my best efforts, nothing I did helped. Eventually, her pain became too unbearable. With much discussion, it was decided that she should have surgery. Little did we know then that a series of unfortunate events surrounding her recovery—not the actual surgery itself—would bring about a tragic and painful end for her and yet another test of my resolve.

Sadly, instead of bringing her home from the hospital after her surgery, Mommy was transferred to a hospice-care facility located right across the street from where my sister had recently moved. I took my anger out on the staff by barking at the nurses if she wasn't clean, and I chased away the male orderlies if they even thought of stepping into her room. I spent hours reading every single Psalm in the Bible to her. I hoped the more devout my heart was, as I read the sacred words, the more that I would find salvation for both of us. But atonement didn't come for either of us.

Thought to be *the day*, all three of my mother's grandchildren lavished her with teary hugs and kisses and said their final goodbyes before they left with my sister. I settled in for what we thought would be the final vigil. The power was out from a recent storm so I had to use a flashlight to read quietly again from the Bible. I mostly concentrated on Psalm 23. Lost within the beautiful words that comforted both of our souls, I nearly leaped out of my chair when Mommy unexpectedly sat up, pointed to the corner of the room, and said, "The man." Ignoring my own fears, I looked around the room with the flashlight. I didn't see anyone else in the room with us, but something didn't feel quite right.

I moved to sit beside Mommy on the bed. Seeking solace, I wrapped my arms securely around her. I stroked her hair and rocked her ever so gently in the quiet darkness like she did for me whenever I was sick as a little girl—like she did for me just recently. Tears of regret dripped softly onto my cheeks, and my heart ached with deceit when I told her that she had our permission if she was ready to go. The pain in my heart intensified as I assured her that I would be all right. I held on to her for the longest time as she labored for even the tiniest of breaths. Near midnight, unconvinced that tonight was *the night*, I gently kissed her forehead and reluctantly returned to my sister's place. It was decided that we would stay at my sister's apartment for the night just in case.

We were roused from our exhausted slumber with the shrill ring of the telephone. I bruised my leg horribly as I stumbled through the unfamiliar darkness toward the sound. The death knoll came at three in the morning. It was the hospice nurse. She told me what I already knew—the angels had taken her home. Mommy was gone. My sister and I threw on our coats and ran across the street to the facility. The atmosphere in her room reminded me of the unordinary stillness of the funeral home. But this time, I wasn't afraid. I lay down beside her, wrapped one arm around her lifeless body, and buried my face into the softness of her hair. I released the tears that I had kept bottled up so as not to have worried her.

After some time, with my soul completely spent, I wiped the tears from my face and whispered consolingly into her ear, "Goodbye, Mommy. Please forgive me. I'm so sorry." Comfortable with our final respects, my sister and I turned and walked solemnly back to her apartment. Silence filled the space between us as we tried to digest what had just occurred. We reached for each other's hand and held on to each other securely—the same way we did as little girls whenever Mommy was taken away from us. Our grasps were even tighter this time because we knew she wouldn't be coming back.

In the midst of all the heartache and confusion, my thirty-eighth birthday came and went. And just when everything seemed to settle back in place, the fifth anniversary of Mark's death reared its ugly head. Without a word to anyone, I closed the blinds, crawled into bed, and prayed for the holidays to be quickly over. I felt even more alone, more alone than ever before. This time, I felt pushed to the limit. My best friend was gone. I felt the familiar comfort of defeat and the willingness to go on weaken in my heart, but I knew I had to. I promised Mommy I would. With the gradual strengthening of my resolve, I felt determined to forge ahead if only by faith and hope.

By a Thread

And so began my tobacco relapse yet again. I smoked off and on in my teens and twenties, but I really kicked the habit for Mark back in '93. I don't think he ever knew because it was a habit that I was ashamed of and, therefore, had kept it to myself. I fell off the wagon not long after Mommy passed away. While the children were away at school one day, I searched maniacally in the garage for Mommy's purse. Rummaging through its contents, I found the very thing I was after—her cigarettes. I took them to the back porch and lit one. Although somewhat stale and nasty tasting, I sealed the deal with an unhealthy habit. A habit that, I hoped, would help me die a somewhat natural death—one that I would only indulge in privately and one that would give me another reason to kick myself.

Like I did before, I went to extremes to hide it from everyone. I had an "I hate smoking" arsenal in my car: a toothbrush and toothpaste, gum, breathe lozenges, a washrag, liquid instant soap, and a bottle of water. And I always had my inhaler nearby. Because I hated the smell and the taste, my cleaning ritual went beyond the obsessive and the ridiculous. Sometimes, I rubbed the skin in and around my mouth raw just to be rid of it. The more opportunities I had to be alone, the more I smoked. The more I smoked, the more I wanted to smoke; and when I couldn't get a moment alone, I became extremely agitated and irritable and had even worse panic attacks.

I went to great lengths to be alone to smoke. I parked behind school buildings, in old abandoned parks, and behind grocery stores to name a few. Somehow, they made me feel better, and yet they made me feel worse at the same time. Eventually, the cravings in the evenings kept me awake; and so I took the risk and began to smoke outside, on our back porch, when my children were asleep. They almost caught me a couple of times. And I don't think I fooled them either; I have never been successful at deceit. Aware that I was presenting a bad example for them made me hate myself even more.

With the possibility that I could live to be a million years old before I would be with either Mommy or Mark again, I convinced myself that if I worked harder, the time would go by faster. So I worked with even more dedicated determination in a variety of odd part-time jobs right through the weekends. When I wasn't working, I busied myself with the children's activities and cleaned the house obsessively. But no matter how much I worked, I couldn't make up for the money that time did not make. Soon I was way over my head financially and was forced to file for bankruptcy. None of it mattered. I didn't care about my credit or much of anything anymore—not even the failing of my health again. I was fixated on the goal to make the time go as fast as possible so I could be with Mark and Mommy again.

With the bankruptcy came the repossession of my car in the middle of the night. Since we lived in an area with limited bus service and the children had extracurricular activities scattered throughout Lynnwood, we were nearly paralyzed without a vehicle. Thankfully, with a loan from the church, I was able to purchase an Uncle Buck station wagon for a thousand dollars. Our home was next. We had to find a less-expensive place to live. Unsurprisingly, and blessed once more, a brand-new two-story townhouse seemed to have dropped from the sky only two blocks from where we currently lived. It was much larger than the duplex we currently lived in. It had a yard, was right on the school-bus line, and cost two hundred dollars less than what we currently were paying. With the help of the church, we zigzagged our way, yet again, back across the speedway.

Battle of the Alamo Revisited

The book resumed to haunt my dreams. This time, it consumed my thoughts throughout the day as well as the night and even more so with every new catastrophe that happened in the world. I cried whenever there was news of another tragedy. I understood only too well the pain of the survivors. It was their pain that cried out to me and motivated me to begin to write, to embark on my journey. For them and for myself, I knew I had to begin the process, but that was easier said than done. Throwing caution to the wind and giving into the will that insisted it should be done, I gave up looking for that elusive permanent job and settled with the occasional part-time temporary job and concentrated on my book. I can't explain it, but every little thing seemed to take care of itself with my brave *leap of faith*. Those close to me were even more convinced I had actually lost my head this time.

To encourage myself, like the town crier, I told everyone and anyone about the book—in the same way I did about Mark—with the premise that the more I spoke of it, the more real it would become. Those who were interested inspired me even further with their enthusiasm of its completion. But it was nearly a year and a half later before I had the nerve to even start. Always with good intentions to begin, I always found a reason or an excuse not to. Rather, I would find some unfinished business that needed tending to. The painful reality of *it* and the fear associated with that reality was more than I could face, and it superseded the motivation I originally had to begin. To fathom the mere possibility that *it* even happened was unbearable. And because the actual writing of the book required a lot of soul-searching, remembering, and processing, it became my most difficult challenge to face and overcome.

I found refuge from that inner turmoil at my weekend job. When I applied for it, I assumed it would be easy—something that I could get lost in. I didn't think it would be difficult to pet dogs for four hours. As a pet nutrition specialist, it was much more than that. I was expected to teach customers the benefits of natural cat and dog food in local pet stores. And I had to brainstorm with them, if their pet had a health care issue, as to what would be a better food choice for them to alleviate their pet's issue. The job was anxiety producing at first. I was used to people approaching me with a concern not vice versa. But within a year and with practice, I became more confident and enjoyed the interactions with the customers. I was in my element. I worked independently, and the animals provided me with a kind of pet therapy. While working, I made friends with fellow coworkers, store employees, and competitors from other pet-food companies. As much as I enjoyed my alone time, being among other living beings was therapy in itself. I finally had a job I could look forward to.

Of the friends I made at one particular pet store, there was a competitor that the others encouraged me to take more notice of. Eventually, I caught on to what they were up to and contemplated their idea. The day I looked into that person of interest's handsome face, my heart skipped a beat. We danced around the feelings between us for another year before either of us had the nerve to make the next move. I was confused by the feelings he stirred within me. After all, my goal was to find a way back to Mark. Never in my wildest dreams had I considered dating someone else. I hadn't even paid much attention to myself since Mark was gone and couldn't contemplate that I was even remotely attractive anymore. The night before another weekend shift, I had a very vivid dream. I couldn't put it out of my mind for the life of me. When I saw him at the pet store later that day, he stopped to say hello, and my face turned as red as a lobster. What I hadn't noticed before was suddenly there. Noticing my stare, he smiled at me with a knowing twinkle in his eye. My breath caught in my throat. I was never as glad as when my shift ended that day. It was obvious our friendship had turned, and it pleased the others to no end. I was excited yet had no idea how to proceed. Part of me wanted this so desperately, but another part of me was scared to death. Throwing caution to the wind, I took the risk and made the first move. I asked him if he had a camera, which he said he did. And then I invited him to Dale's high school graduation.

That was the beginning. Soon we were getting together nearly every evening for dessert and coffee. We felt comfortable in one another's company and never ran out of things to talk or laugh about. Occasionally, when we met at his place, he would entice me to dance with him. Awkward yet exciting at the same time—born without rhythm or dancing feet compared to his years as a professional salsa dancer—he was patient and comical as I stumbled over his feet while trying to keep up with his lead. It seemed odd to be in the arms of someone other than Mark. Our music of choice was Natalie Cole's album *Unforgettable, With Love*. We dubbed the song "That Sunday, That Summer" as our song since we had met during the summer on a Sunday. He was very much the opposite of Mark especially in size and stature. He stood only a head taller than me, and my arms could reach all the way around him. Although just a year older than Mark, he seemed much younger. Born of Mexican descent and a spitting image of Cheech Marin, impeccable in his taste for food and the way he dressed—dress slacks only since he hates blue jeans—he was also the complete opposite of me. With his demeanor, the way he spoke—with a thick Spanish accent—and the respect he had for women, he was very much a courteous and honorable man. His favorite music was opera and nothing else; he especially liked Alfredo Kraus and Pavarotti. Despite our differences, we clicked like two missing pieces of a jigsaw puzzle.

Of all the things I would share with him, I touched lightly on the subject of Mark. And the more I avoided that subject, the more intrigued and persistent he became to pursue it. He knew only too well how much I hurt because he too had lost his one and only true love. Over twenty years before, his young wife died tragically in a horrific car accident as she passed over a railway and right into the path of an oncoming train. He also received the devastating news while he was at work. He never remarried nor had any children. He came to the United States alone a few years after her death, penniless and affluent only in Spanish with the knowledge of few English words, and made a new life for himself in Seattle. He was satisfied with his autonomy. We had something in common—something so profound that only a fellow traveler, on the same journey, could comprehend the complexity of that turning point in one's life.

Chapter Four: The Journey Begins

It took him several years to face his own reality and to begin to heal. Aware of the consequences of denial and because he cared enough about me, he made it his mission—or obsession—that I begin the journey that I so wanted to avoid. His lure was through my book. He encouraged me constantly to begin. All the while, he chiseled inconspicuously and determinedly at the fortress around my heart where I kept Mark alive. And one evening, he succeeded. Finishing our dessert and coffee, he nonchalantly brought up *the subject* again. Angry and frustrated with his constant meddling, fighting the urge to cry, I stood up and walked into his living room so he couldn't see my reaction. But somehow he knew. Somehow he always knew. He approached me and gently wrapped his arms around me. His masculine yet compassionate embrace tugged at the chains surrounding my inner fortress. In that brief moment, I became aware of the depth of my own suffering. The buried thoughts, feelings, and sensations I once held hostage and fought so fiercely to keep at bay refused to be beaten down this time. He turned me around to face him. I looked into the never-ending depths of his soft brown eyes, and my reserve broke. A sob forced its way to the surface and then another and another and others—thick and fast. Up and up they came to the surface for release despite my unwillingness to let it happen. He held me in his arms even tighter. I gave up the struggle and let myself cry freely, helplessly, and openly. It was all over; I was sure that I had lost what I could hardly say that I had found. But rather than recoiling, he held me even closer and whispered reassuringly, "I am on your side, Elise. I believe in you, and I will be here whenever you need me."

His unbendable perseverance astounded yet intrigued me; I had met my match. He was not easily dissuaded by any of the hundreds of excuses I came up with not to begin writing the book—my seeming fragility or the fact that most of the information I needed to begin was in *the box*. With or without my cooperation, plans were soon underway to resurrect it. To plan was one thing; to carry out the plan was another. I delayed the event as long as I could. Again he wasn't fooled nor put off by my purposeful procrastination. And one Saturday, after I finished work, he escorted me personally to my house to oversee the exhumation and transfer of *the box* to his house. I was dumbfounded when I walked into his home. He not only had his living room prepared in advance for the dreaded impending event, but an inviting lunch awaited us as well. I delayed finishing my meal as long as possible. Immune to my dawdling, he got straight to work as soon as he finished, announcing with business-like purpose, "Come on, let's get started."

I felt the color drain from my face when I looked across the room at *the box*. I felt a familiar and foreboding sense of dread, and panic began to spread like wild ivy inside my chest. My legs felt like lead. I couldn't find the strength to move from my chair. More than ever before I wanted to leave. Sensing my reaction, he gingerly linked my arm with his; and in silent reverence, we walked together and approached *the box*. We worked nonstop and silently side by side, sorting and making various piles of things—media videos, newspaper clippings, condolence cards, pictures, etc. I was amazed by the amount of the things I had gathered over the years. From memory, he labeled the names of each of the chapters on boxes and envelopes from each of the piles. His genuine concern for something so important to me touched my heart deeply. If he was out to earn his wings—like Clarence from my favorite movie *It's a Wonderful Life*—he certainly was on the right path. Eventually, I found the special glass frame that held my Safeway flowers. As I carefully unwrapped and rewrapped it, it occurred to me that while I had spent a lot of time and effort protecting and preserving some of Mark's most sentimental things, I had totally ignored and abused his most precious treasure of all—me. With that profound revelation, I wept silently to myself. Lost in the memories, I continued to sort through the piles. Like the wrath of the sea, waves of emotion rippled and crashed down upon me. One minute, I found myself crying; and the next minute, something would make me laugh. I felt hostage to the grey obscurity of reality. Soon evening cast its shadow over the room. We finished by the dim light of a lamp he brought in from somewhere else.

From outside the reverent silence, his familiar soothing voice broke through the grey barrier. "We're finished, Elise, you did it!" In disbelief, I just stared at him, and then I laughed. He took me in his arms and told me how proud he was of me. And then I lost it again. "He's gone," I cried. As the realization seeped into my very being, I cried even harder. Like a break in a dam, I couldn't stop. I hadn't cried that hard since Mark's viewing. My throat ached; my eyes hurt. I held on to him even tighter as my knees buckled from beneath me. "He's really gone, Roberto . . ."

*   *   *

Two Days Later

I am returning to continue writing after two days of procrastination for fear of what happened while writing the above-unfinished sentence. As I was typing, I noticed that the letters I was hitting were not the same letters appearing on the page. I fought with the keyboard. I purposely made the effort to press the correct keys, but it wouldn't cooperate. When I pushed the apostrophe key, a quotation mark would appear. When I tried to move a series of highlighted words to another place, they became scrambled. When I tried to capitalize a letter, the Shift key would make it lowercase with and without the Caps Lock on. And then when I tried a final time to move the cursor into the correct position, it just took off. Whole paragraphs began to highlight off and on. The keyboard and the computer were out of control; it seemed as though it had been hijacked.

The hair on the back of my neck stood up; the skin on my body erupted in goose bumps. Instinctively, I picked up the phone and called my sister. I sobbed to her hysterically about what was happening. Spooked, she told me to save my work if I could and turn off the computer. She suggested that I get away from the book for a while, to go outside and enjoy the sunshine. After I calmed down and we hung up, I went to collect my shoes and purse. As I turned to leave the room, large snapping flames of static electricity began to shoot out from the HEPA filter on the dresser, rattling my nerves even more. I turned it off quickly and ran out of the house. Beyond shaken, I nearly left skid marks in the driveway as

I sped away. The following day, I brought the HEPA filter to the store where I bought it earlier that year. They said it was beyond repair and that they couldn't figure out how or why. The next day, I continued with my story.

*   *   *

My heart hurt as seven years of pent-up emotion crashed through the so-called dam of steel I had built around it. The wounded animal cry, which I had learned to suppress, found its way out in my cries. When my knees gave way, Roberto held me even tighter. "It's okay, honey. It's okay. Let it go. You have to let it go." Gathering the fabric from his shirt tightly in the grasp of my fingers and holding on to him as though my life depended on it, I cried even harder. Staying the course, he continued to whisper reassuringly into my ear. Sometime later, emotionally spent and exhausted, he wiped the tears from my face. With swollen eyes and a red nose, I smiled up at him and kissed him gently. Captivated by the depths of his deep brown eyes, I saw a familiar friend within my reflection, and I knew everything was going to be all right. He continued to hold me securely, waiting for the signal to let go. My soul stirred. I felt a transformation beginning in my heart. In his arms, I felt safe. I wanted to stay there forever. He returned my kiss, stirring the sleeping winter in my soul, melting away long-held feelings of fearfulness, guilt, and despair, and replacing them with life and love once more. I snuggled closer to him. For the first time in a long time, I felt hopeful.

I felt lighter after dealing with the box. But it was only one of the many hurdles of *acceptance* I had yet to face before I could begin to write. The following weekend, curled up next to Roberto—apprehensive of the following sequence of events—with his arms securely around me and a box of tissue at hand, we watched each and every video I had collected. He held me even tighter if I happened to sob or sigh deeply. In each video, there was one consistent message. It pounded its way into my heart and my brain mercilessly. *It* really happened, and Mark *was* really gone. With each video, the message seemed easier to digest, and I began to feel a little stronger. To keep up the pace, we dedicated every weekend to the book. The next task was to sort through all of the typewritten articles of the tragedy that I had collected. As I pulled a pile out of the box labeled 11-27-98, an audio cassette fell out and onto my lap. I laughed as I recalled the session with Ralph. Excitedly, I brought it to Roberto. He put into the cassette player. With intense curiosity, we listened. Our hearts virtually stood still with the last prediction Ralph made.

He paused as if listening to something and then muttered "Martin." Asking aloud who this was, he said the name again, "Oh Martin!" Muttering again, shaking his head with utmost certainty, he said, "It's either part of his first or last name." After a moment, he exclaimed, with even more certainty, "It is most definitely a part of his last name!" Confused, I asked whose last name he was referring to. He said matter-of-factly, "It is the name of the man you will marry someday, but not for a long while."

In disbelief, we rewound the tape. Practically holding our breath, we put our ears closer to the speaker and listened again to the prophecy. Afterward, we sat for a brief time, in the deafening silence, in awe of what possibly could or could not be. My eyes met with his. The most wonderful and incredible man before me was none other than Roberto *Martinez*. Whether it was pure coincidence or divine intervention through both of our beloveds, I laughed a genuine laugh for the first time in seven years and joyfully wrapped my arms around my hero and planted a great big kiss on his cheek. He laughed as he returned my kiss and said, "See, I told you it was meant to be." Some never find true love. Some only find it once. We knew we were blessed to have found it twice. Ralph's revelation was all we needed to break the ice. All too familiar with the risks of almost certain loss in a world of impermanence, we dove headfirst with our eyes wide-open. Very much aware that tomorrow may never come, we made a vow to love each other to the fullest extent that day and every day thereafter. It felt odd loving more than one person at the same time, but the four of us were content just the same. No longer a solitary traveler, I felt brave enough to take the first steps on my journey.

The Impossible Dream

*T*he bubble surrounding our happiness nearly burst in my face the day I confessed my clandestine affair with the Marlboro man to Roberto. The disappointment in his eyes was apparent. I felt deeply ashamed. He proposed an ultimatum. Either it was him or the cigarettes. He wouldn't hang around to watch me kill myself. He was a no-nonsense man and true to his word. Shocked, I understood what I had to do. It wasn't until I attempted to put the nasty things out of my life did I realize that I had become addicted to them again. Armed with some holistic calming aids, lots of mints, and gum, making certain that I was rarely alone for the first two weeks, I quit cold turkey. It was hell, but I would rather have walked over hot coals before losing Roberto. Ironically, as time progressed as a nonsmoker, my panic attacks gradually dissipated.

The book kept my mind busy as I sorted through mounds of material, highlighting important facts and shredding duplicate information. Archiving the rest back to the box, I eventually forgot all about *them* and kept focused on the task at hand. As I researched the material—like the videos—the more I read, the more the message drove home and the stronger I became. While I organized the momentous amount of information, Roberto prepared a desk for me right next to his. He furnished it with the things I needed: pens, pencils, a dictionary, a thesaurus, an endless supply of candles, and other essentials. The most thoughtful of these were two prayer books. And lastly, he armed an archaic computer that he no longer used with the latest Windows software he had. With all the prep work done, I was ready to write, or so I thought. Sitting at my desk for the first time, with a blank Word 2003 page staring at me challengingly, I felt absolutely lost. I didn't know where to begin. Always in tune with my feelings, Roberto dimmed the lights, placed some lit candles around my desk, put the two prayer books in my hands and suggested I pray for guidance, and then left me on my own.

And I did pray. I prayed with all my heart for guidance, for Him—in all of his infinite glory along with his angels—to give me the words that would help not only myself, but also those who would read my story to heal. But something still wasn't right. Roberto returned. I explained that it was too quiet and asked if he had some music without words. It was as though he had all the tools that I required waiting nearby for my request. He put on a soundtrack from an older movie, *Somewhere in Time*, that I enjoyed and set it to play repeatedly. I never tired of the same music even after hearing it play over and over for hours and hours. It inspired me and filled me with hope. Unexplainably, from the first time I placed my fingers into position on the keyboard and as if transcribing from a recorder, the words would pour out onto the *paper.* The experience was indescribable. With each blessed word, the links in the chain surrounding my heart would fall one by one, taking the heaviness in my soul along with them. The release was unimaginable and captivating. I wanted to stay in that moment forever. The words came whether I was ready or not. Like Mickey Mouse and the Magic Brooms from the movie *Fantasia,* they were unstoppable. Momentous and strong, they forced themselves through my fingers. Incessant, they haunted my nighttime dreams more than the book ever had until I wrote them down. I wrote for hours at a time, oblivious to the carpal tunnel in my wrists. The first thirteen thousand words were written in nine consecutive days.

My writing ritual remained unchanged. To me, it was sacred. So much, in fact, I couldn't begin the process without the candles, the music, or the prayers and prayer books. They filled me with the peace and quiet discipline I required to listen and heal. Throughout the writing of the book, I was sometimes so overwhelmed that I had to leave my writing for the day. Sometimes I could only write for an hour at a time. Sometimes I avoided the writing process altogether for several days before I had the nerve to face *it* again in spite of the nightmares. It took several months to process through the first and third chapters because of the harsh reality between their pages. If my fear delayed the writing process, I was besieged by further nightmares of the horrifying events that lurked in each of them. And only when I surrendered and resumed writing could I rest peacefully. The thoughts, the process, and the pain were sometimes so unbearable I wasn't sure if I would ever finish the book. Yet throughout its creation, Roberto pushed me when I didn't want to budge and cheered me onward as it progressed.

And then there was the constant struggle to balance writing with earning a living. But as expected, Roberto had an answer for that dilemma too. He offered me a job. He had a small business that didn't get the attention it needed because of the demands of his full-time job. I wouldn't have a salary per se or the perks of a regular job—as the business wasn't very profitable—but he would help me pay my bills as they came. He said I could make it my baby if I wanted to accept. Without reservation, I jumped on the opportunity, and I became the official vice president of his CEDAR-AL business. Because it wasn't demanding, I was able to balance working for Roberto and the writing of the book. It was the perfect job. For the second time, Roberto and I worked side by side and eventually resurrected the business, which gradually improved the profits. Ironically, like writing the book, I had no prior training; but technical knowledge seemed natural to me. With prayer and patience—the business becoming a part of my daily meditation—I created a Web site for the business. It has a women's touch with bright colors, animated bugs, and plenty of informative material to read. Although frustrating at times, it was fun. With the sales and marketing experience I acquired from various jobs as a demonstrator, our products were soon on the shelves of over twenty-five western Washington stores including one in New York and one in Florida. We set a goal, one day, to have them on the shelves of at least one retailer from the remaining forty-seven states. With the new Web site, we were able to reach international customers too with a regular from the Netherlands. Eventually, I assumed the role of Roberto's account and bookkeeping manager, personal as well as professional. Working for Roberto filled me with a sense of purpose and accomplishment—more so than any other job I ever had.

Chapter Four: The Journey Begins

Of the support I had while writing, the most entertaining was from Roberto's cat—who is, of course, the business mascot—a handsome and gentle tuxedo Norwegian Forest cat named Lucky. Every day, Lucky took his post by my side when I arrived for work. With dutiful purpose and loving encouragement, he would sit tirelessly—sometimes for hours—beside me while I wrote only to relinquish his post upon Roberto's arrival home. If I had an especially emotional writing day, he would jump into my arms, wrap his little paws around my neck, and purr consolingly until he was assured that the storm had passed. My goal was to finish the book by Roberto's birthday, eleven months later to be exact. But 2006 quickly passed by and with it went Roberto's birthday and the book still wasn't finished. The ending remained unwritten. As always, Roberto knew just what had to be done.

The following weekend, Lexi, Roberto, and I took a little field trip. The wind blew hard and cold into our faces as Lex led the way to the *place of origin*. She stopped when she reached the concrete pillar that encased Mark's memorial plaque. I reached out and touched it. I touched the railing and felt the newness of the pieces that replaced the ones torn away that fateful day. I looked over the bridge and to the top of the apartment. My heart skipped a beat as I recognized Mark's final resting place from the noticeably large replaced sections of the roof. My heart ached as I thought about how frightened he must have been. I couldn't believe the distance between the bridge and the apartment. Lost in the thought of how that day horrible day must have unfolded, Roberto squeezed my arm, bringing me back to the security of the present time. I pulled him closer.

Placing my hand on the memorial plaque once again, I closed my eyes and whispered a silent farewell to Mark, "Goodbye, Hunny Bunny, my best friend, my love." Each word stuck in my throat. My eyes burned as the tears fell, and I continued, "I will never love you any less. I will still care deeply for you forever, but from this day forward, I must and will be going it alone." As I let my hand slip slowly away from the pillar, it seemed as though the sadness in my heart and the weight on my shoulders were lifted, caught up in the current of the breeze, floating away with the words I spoke. I smiled to myself. I was free at last. I was lost no more. My journey was complete. I whispered quietly to Roberto and Lexi that I was ready to go. Lex led the way. With our backs to the never more dark and ominous bridge, we walked away toward a new beginning in our lives. As if in silent revere, bus route number 358 zoomed quietly by, blanketing us with a warm and comforting breeze.

But my story doesn't end there. As fresh as a newly engraved headstone, the day of Mark's death remains permanently etched in the not-so-far corner of my mind, and the healing process continues. Sometimes it's day by day. Ironically, the answers I had prayed so desperately before were available to me all along—in the love and support of my friends and family, in the writing of this book, and above all, in *acceptance*.

Bonus Story: Spiritual Intervention

Spirit, 2000

*R*ecently a widowed bride and my children being the only reason for me to get out of bed and face the world each day, I found it helpful—in the attempt to avoid the suffocating and overwhelming feelings of grief—to dive headfirst into several projects. I just wanted to be busy and forget. Preparing the new home I had recently bought for us was the most time-consuming of them all. I wasn't handy with tools, and I lacked the redecorating skills required for the expectations my imagination conjured up. Naive of how much effort the work called for, I forged blindly ahead. Every night, after dinner, I drove to the new house and spent several hours single-handedly scrubbing, wallpapering, and painting. When I accomplished as much as I could, I would drive back to our apartment in time to catch a few hours of sleep before going to work the next day.

Since there wasn't anyone available who could help me with what had become a very big project, it wasn't long before frustration, impatience, and exhaustion had me in their grips. The fourth week into my project, I began to feel the dizzying effects of the hamster treadmill I had put myself on. One evening, as I stood in the center of the living room—the last room to be cleaned and painted—and gazed in awe at the height of the cathedral ceilings and the length of the walls, all my pent-up feelings came to a head. Overwhelmed and overcome, I collapsed into a fit of weeping emotion. I cried like I've never cried before. I hit the floor with my fists and screamed *why* and cried, "I can't do this all by myself!" Until I couldn't cry, sob, or pound any more. Exhausted, I sat in a heap and prayed. Sitting there a while longer, I decided that the living room would have to wait until the following day and called it a night. I pulled myself together and drove home. Needless to say, I completed the living room by the end of the same week, and I have to admit that I did a pretty good job too!

I found moving in more fun than redecorating. So much fun, in fact, I found myself so consumed by the task that I forgot about my prayer vigil, but little did I know that answers had already been conceived and were on their way. This story is about one of those many wonderful blessings we received that brought us hope. It was the end of summer of 1999. We lived in our new home for nearly a month when, one day, my daughter ran into the house—nearly out of breath—and announced excitedly, "Mama, Mama, you have to see what Sasha has!" She pulled me toward the front door where Sasha—her new neighborhood friend—stood. Laughing all the way, I followed her, expecting to see some unexciting thing. Sasha approached me, cradling something as equally tiny as her hands. Then she offered me some sort of a black and fuzzy animal. I couldn't tell what it was at first. It was so small. With a nub for a tail, I thought it was a hamster.

In desperation, Sasha pleaded, "Can you save this kitty? Its mother has killed its four brothers and sisters, and I just got this one away from her as she was biting on it. She bit its tail off, see, and your daughter says you're a nurse. And I was wondering if you could save him." My daughter was jumping up and down and begging me at this point. At the time, I wasn't a practicing nurse, and my specialty definitely wasn't in the veterinary field. Hesitantly, I scooped the tiny thing into my hands. As I held the tiny creature, the warmth from its little body radiated through my hands, traveled up through my arms and my chest, and straight into my heart. My motherly instincts took over. I gave him a quick one-minute examination and determined *it* was a he, and although his eyes and ears were closed, he appeared to be no worse for wear.

He was so tiny and vulnerable. I was certain caring for him couldn't be any harder than mothering or nursing. Without hesitation, I hurried into the house in search of a towel to wrap him in. As I passed by my daughter, I heard her shout yeah behind me. I wrapped him gingerly with a thick cotton bath towel, climbed carefully into my truck, tucked him safely into my lap, and headed for the vet who cares for our other cats. Once there, I learned of his fate. The vet said he had only a 30 percent chance of surviving as he weighed at only two ounces. She shared her concern for my recent loss and my ability to handle the additional grief if he didn't survive. She strongly recommended that we find someone else to take on the responsibility of helping him. Inwardly, I argued with her rationale. I just couldn't abandon him. Not now. With the persistence of a pleading child, I assured her that I could handle the responsibility no matter what the outcome. Somewhat unconvinced, she reluctantly pulled out her pen and wrote down the instructions of how to care for him.

As is my usual stubborn nature, I chose to deny the reality of how much work and time—as I had in redecorating of the house—caring for this little creature involved. With my maternal instincts in full bore, I wrapped him in the towel once again and headed for the pet store. I bought kitten formula, a tiny syringe, and a kitten-care booklet. While bagging my purchases, the friendly clerk offered me some helpful hints. Ironically, I felt like I did when I was a new mother; everyone wants to see the new baby and give you their best theories of how to care for it. After I arrived home, I quickly read through the important sections in the kitten book. It suggested he have a quiet, warm, dark place to sleep and a windup clock close to him so he would think he was with his mother. And then I set out on a scavenger hunt for all the other things he required. First, I found a small cat carrier in my garage and prepared a little nest inside it with an old sweatshirt of mine. Next, I found a hot water bottle, filled it with warm water, and wrapped it in a small kitchen towel. And lastly, I found a windup clock and wound it tightly until it was ticking at a fairly fast pace. Then the fun began.

I followed the instructions on the canister of kitten formula to make a batch of milk. Having breast-fed my children, this bottle-making stuff was totally foreign to me. I pierced a hole on the top of the nipple of the tiny bottle with a sharp sewing needle. Following the vet's instructions, I propped him up in a semisitting position in my hand and put the bottle in his mouth. Feeding him was as challenging as it was scary. And no matter how big of a hole I poked in the nipple, he couldn't find satisfaction. Finally—after several attempts with the bottle—we both gave up and settled with a needle-less syringe a pharmacist once gave me. At first, I worried that I was pushing the plunger too fast. I thought he would surely drown. But not to worry, the little piglet sucked the plunger down faster than I could push it. He seemed content with how much the syringe could feed him at one time and what little effort it required of him. Initially, I worried he was eating too much as the instructions indicated he should only be fed a certain amount to a certain ounce in weight. But he was the exception to their rules. He ate until he was full—his belly nearly bursting like an overfilled water balloon—sometimes taking in twice as what was recommended. But I let him be the judge of how much food he needed. I assured myself that it was the right thing to do, certain his cat mother would have done the same. Amazingly, he ate by the syringe, in supersized quantities, every three to four hours.

Continuing to follow the vet's instructions, I turned him on his stomach and wiped his bottom until he eliminated. I discovered that this also made him burp. I was as excited as a new mother. Until the toileting process became messier. Sometimes I didn't have enough tissue to sop up everything, and it would end up on me. Eventually, my hands blistered from continuous hand washing, every three to four hours before and after feeding and toileting him. Assured he had a full belly, I cleaned him up, kissed the top of his tiny head—the beginning of what became our nightly ritual—and put him to bed inside of the carrier, on top of my old shirt, and next to the warm towel-wrapped water bottle. Comforted by its warmth, he instinctively curled up next to it. Contented by the rhythmic sound of the windup clock ticking beside him, he was lulled to sleep instantly. Nestled within his carrier on the throw rug next to the head of my bed he slept, oblivious to the cruel world from which he had been saved. I snuggled down in my own bed and prayed that the little nest would suffice for the mother that wasn't there.

The first night, we fell asleep quickly and soundly. But it was short-lived. He awoke for a feeding promptly three hours later. And usually, nothing but the shrill ring from an alarm clock or the cry from one of my children could wake me from a sound sleep, but this little kitty could. He had a meow louder than he was big. So barely awake with one eye open—mumbling under my breath a vow to never have another baby, human or animal—and cradling the screaming baby kitty, I stumbled into the kitchen and prepared the necessary apparatus for his midnight snack. Eventually, I learned to prepare everything—including an extra batch or two of formula—prior to our bedtime. With just the glow from the overhead stove lamp and his feeding and toileting arsenal at hand, I sat on the rug in the middle of the kitchen floor and began what would become another nightly ritual for weeks to come. It took nearly an hour to get him ready for bed again as well as an additional ten minutes warming up his water bottle and changing his soiled bed. But once we were nestled in our beds for a second time, falling asleep again was easy for both of us—him from a full tummy and me from new kitty-mommy anxiety and pure exhaustion.

The kitten posed another dilemma for me. I had to work the following Monday. I called around but couldn't find anyone to take on the responsibilities he required in an eight-hour workday let alone for the next month or two of workdays. I was forced to call my boss. Thankfully, she didn't have a problem with my *newborn* coming to work with me and suggested that he stay in the conference room while I worked. When Monday morning arrived, I awoke earlier than usual to get both of us ready on time. I packed my lunch and a makeshift diaper bag with his feeding and toileting apparatus. Since it was early fall and the mornings were becoming chilly, I wrapped him warmly in one of my daughter's doll blankets. Balancing my cumbersome load, I hollered after-school instructions to my children and walked out the door. It was awkward carrying so much stuff the three long country blocks to the bus stop. I wished I still had a baby stroller, but that would have bothered the other commuters on the bus. "Oh well," I sighed as I thought about doing this for the next three weeks, "we'll live through this." Once at the bus stop, I set my load down and reached into my purse for my bus pass but found something wet instead. The kitten milk I packaged and fit into my purse so nicely had spilled. I panicked. He couldn't survive an entire day without his milk, and kitten milk wasn't readily available at the corner store. I had no other choice but to trudge all the way home and make some more. In a sweaty, frustrated hurry, I cleaned out my purse. I made a new batch of milk and packaged it in securer container. Because I missed my scheduled bus, I had to drive to the nearest park and ride to catch another one. It was a miracle I made it to work on time.

At my office, the kitten was the main attraction. My coworkers watched with anticipation as he grew and thrived. It was a cause for celebration at work and at home when he opened his eyes and ears for the first time and when he took his first steps. Day by day, he became bigger and stronger and continued to gain an ounce or three on a weekly basis. The vet was pleased with how well he was thriving. She congratulated me for the kitten's successful recovery and assured me that he would survive. The kitten also adjusted well to the daily hour-and-a-half bus ride to and from work. He kept the fellow commuters amused with his growth and development milestones. Eventually, he began to protest his confinement in the carrier. He was loud, and—like a baby—holding him was the only way to quiet him regardless of the policies on the bus. Risking a long walk home, I had to harbor him in the folds of my jacket or put my hand in the carrier to console him. In my heart, I knew it was time to leave him at home; but since he still seemed so young, I decided to wait an additional week or two before attempting it.

When the time came, I organized his care routine around my work schedule and my children's school schedule. At first, I was somewhat unconvinced that the kitten was ready to be handled by my nearly teenage children—as the toileting task really disgusted them—but they proved to be just as cautious and careful with him as I was and gradually required less and less kitty-care instructions over the phone. Without incident, my morning commute returned to normal. For a while, my cocommuters and coworkers really missed the kitten. Spending most of his early life en route, he expected to be taken along whenever the family went out. One Saturday, I took him with me while I had lunch with my sister. She doted and gushed over him. She paraded him around her work area and showed him to all her coworkers. She even insisted that she be the one to feed and toilet him. That's just the type of auntie she is.

Bonus Story: Spiritual Intervention

During our luncheon, my sister asked if I had chosen a name for the kitten. Embarrassed, I admitted that an appropriate name for him hadn't caught my attention yet. She observed that since I had the kitten, I had become a different person—almost like my old self before Mark died. The mention of Mark invited grief to engulf me in its grips once again. A lump formed in my throat as she continued. I nuzzled the kitten for comfort, burying my face into his fur and fighting the urge to cry. She said she believed Mark sent him for me. Her comment shocked me; she had always denied the possibility of such a thing. The thought of Mark continuing to be concerned for me made my eyes burn and swell with tears. She continued. She said the kitty should have an angelic, guardian sort of name and then suggested he be named Spirit. Tears splashed down my cheeks. I cried for my angelic gift and for Mark. I could only nod in agreement that Spirit was a perfect name. A kitty who cheats death and brings hope to a grieving family must indeed be a divine spirit.

Two summers came and went. All the while, Spirit hurtled many milestones and obstacles along the way and literally grew in leaps and bounds. The vet predicted he would eventually weigh fifteen pounds, but he fooled him. Full grown, he weighed a little over twenty pounds! It made me wonder what was in that kitty formula anyway. While he grew, his body matured faster than his head did. For a while, I worried about my disproportionate, pinheaded kitty; but rest assured, he eventually grew into himself. Thankfully, his kitty developmental skills came to him instinctively. The litter box was a no-brainer, and he learned to walk while trying to keep up with my feet as I scooted backward. The stronger and more sure-footed he became, the faster I had to scoot, and it wasn't long before he was chasing after me. The larger he grew, the lazier he became when he walked. He put his weight into every single step he took. Lacking the stealth-like quiet, pitter-patter, and social graces of a cat, he was an unlikely candidate as a cat burglar. With a horse-like clipity-clop, Spirit's steps echoed mine whenever he trotted alongside me. He kept time with my shadow anywhere and everywhere I went and dutifully waited at my feet if I sat. When he wasn't following me, it was expected that he was hiding somewhere, waiting to ambush me the moment I walked by. Although I knew he was going to fly out of nowhere and tackle my ankles from behind, he still scared me half to death whenever he did it. I'm certain that my dramatic reactions to these surprise attacks were what encouraged him to keep up the little game he created.

Overall, he developed normally—with the exception of his more dog-like than cat-like character. Rather than cat toys, he found it more entertaining to play and chew on things lying around the house. His chew toys of choice were shoes, my slippers, and soft CD case covers. Priceless treasures too precious to chew were hidden: hair bands, candy, paper, and many other things we thought we lost. His favorite hiding spot was underneath my son's bed. We always got a good laugh from what we found there, especially when his loot mostly consisted of my cough drops. I'll never forget the first time I caught him stealing them. Somehow he opened my toiletries drawer, climbed in, and nearly fished out a cherry cough drop from a bag when I startled him. The bag remained stuck over his face when he popped his head out of the drawer. The remaining drops cascaded down his body like an upset apple cart. I never laughed as hard as I did that day.

Like a dog, Spirit was very vocal. He greeted us with a hearty meow when we arrived home. He complained and whined if we shut him out of a room we were in, namely the bathroom. He whined when he was hungry or when he wanted a bite of what we were eating. And he whined when he wanted to be taken along if we went somewhere. He was even worse in the mornings. If we didn't get up when our alarms went off, he'd bump, scratch, and rattle the door nearly off its hinges until we opened it to assure him we were up. And he absolutely flipped if I happened to yell or cry. Also like a dog, he assumed guard duty every night as the family slept. Rather than sleep on the comfy sofa in the living room, he'd sleep on the hard floor in the hallway between our bedrooms. With his head resting on his outstretched paws, lying a bit on his side, ears at attention, dozing lightly, we could count on him to be at the ready to meow incessantly and break down our doors with any unfamiliar noise including falling leaves and thunderstorms. And while on duty—like an unmovable marble statue—he wouldn't budge not even if we accidentally stumbled over him to get to the bathroom. He was even more vigilant whenever we were ill, especially if my son and I had bouts of asthmatic coughing. He insisted we keep our bedroom doors open at night so he could check on us. If we forgot, he'd keep everyone awake with his worrisome yowling, bumping, scratching, and rattling of the doors until we opened them again.

True to his loyalty, he seemed to know when I felt sad or lonely or missed Mark the most. He'd stand on his two hind legs, lean on me with one paw, reach out to me with the other, and meow as if to say "I'm here." And when I picked him up, he'd wrap his giant gentle paws around my neck and let me hug and hold him as tightly as I needed to. And as always, whenever I felt the need to cry, he would allow me to bury my face into his soft furry neck until the storm passed. All the while, he'd purr loudly and consolingly into my ear, unconcerned about how wet my tears made him or how constricted my hugs were. Words can never describe the love I felt for this one-in-a-million and irreplaceable kitty.

Spirit's third summer—Mark's birthday to be exact—began one cool evening with Spirit escaping out the front door. Always hoping for an out through the incoming traffic, his efforts finally paid off, and he was free from the confines of the inside. I panicked and chased after him, but—faster than any free bird could fly—he was gone. I called for him at hourly intervals, but he didn't come home. I went to bed and didn't sleep a wink ever vigilant for his meowing or scratching on the door, but none came. In the morning, I searched and called for him again, but he still didn't come. Hurrying my daughter to leave for her school bus, we were interrupted by a commotion toward the front of the house. It was some of my daughter's school friends running up our front steps and ringing our doorbell frantically. I came to the door to see what the matter was. They were breathless and appeared as if something had frightened them. In between breaths, they begged me to come to the bus stop and muttered something about finding Spirit and took off down the street.

With dread in my heart, I ran after them. I felt a sense of déjà vu as I approached the bus stop. Spirit was lying motionless on the sidewalk. But I didn't see Spirit; I saw Mark lying there in his place. Oblivious to the stares from the children on the school bus and our neighbors, I screamed and collapsed into a weeping heap at Spirit's side. A blanket was offered to me. I gathered him within its folds—just as I had done three years before—and held him closely as I gingerly carried him home. I placed him in the backseat of my truck and went to tell my daughter. She could tell, from the familiar look on my face, something was terribly wrong. "What?" she asked with desperation. "What's wrong, Mommy?"

With her friends watching, I took her in my arms, knowing the news I had to tell would break her little heart. In between tears, I told her—as gently as I could—that Spirit died. Shocked, she screamed *no* and burst into tears. Holding on to me tighter, she cried for a while more. My daughter held Spirit in her lap while I drove her friends to school. Her tears rained gently down onto his silky fur. I excused her from school, and we took Spirit to the nearest animal hospital. Grief stricken, we surrendered him to the staff, but I just couldn't *discard* him. The staff told us about a man, who lived in the community, that cremated pets and made special pine boxes to hold their ashes in. I agreed; it was just what we wanted. Within a week, Spirit was given back to us in his own special box. He continues to rest in peace on the dresser next to my bed alongside his and Mark's photo. Spirit and I were each other's guardian angels. Brought together in our most desperate hours, we saved each other from uncertain fates. He kept me from wallowing in depression, and I gave him life-sustaining care. Above all, we gave each other unconditional love. Although our time together was brief, I will always be grateful for my heaven-sent gift.

Afterword

*A*s evident by my story, I am not a poster child for grief. It took me seven years to even *accept* the fact that *it* really happened. I've learned there is no right or wrong way to go through grief and that it cannot be outrun—it has to be faced head on. And that the stages come and go in no particular sequence. Like the ebb and flow of tide, each and every wave must be ridden to make some progress forward. Most importantly, I've learned that of all the steps, the most important—yet the most difficult—is the stage of acceptance. But it is the only one that will open the doors toward healing. Learning how to grieve and letting myself grieve has freed me to live and to attach again. Through it all, I've gained the confidence I can handle both life and death. And with that security, I am better able to share my affection fully and completely. I've learned valuable lessons I never wanted to learn: about the value of life, faith, and self-discovery. Mark promised me the children and I would always be loved and taken care of; he continues to keep his promise.

About The Author

At press time, Elise and Roberto reside in Lynnwood, Washington, with their four cats—Sniffles, Lucky, Foxy, and Fluke. Their CEDAR-AL business continues to flourish and prosper. Her son, Dale, is currently serving in the United States Navy as an aviation ordinance man. His ultimate goal is to become a Navy SEAL. He plans to make the Navy his career. Her daughter, Lexi, lives in southwest Washington, works full-time in a bank, and attends a technical college full-time. Her ultimate goal is to become an architectural engineer. *A Promise Kept* is Elise's first book; "Spiritual Intervention" was her first short story prior to the writing of this book. She is currently working on *Wednesday's Child,* a prequel to *A Promise Kept.*

Index

LaVergne, TN USA
10 December 2009
166570LV00003B/190/P

9 781441 510389